These Are My Flowers

These Are My Flowers

Raising a Family on the Big Sur Coast

Letters of Nancy Hopkins

Edited by Heidi Hopkins

With historical photos from the 1950s

Poems on pages 66–67 and 104 reprinted with permission from the Big Sur Historical Society

Excerpt on page 140 by Henry Miller, from *Big Sur and the Oranges of Hieronymus Bosch*,
copyright © 1957 by New Directions Publishing Corp.
Reprinted by permission of New Directions Publishing Corp.

Photography credits:
Page 52: Charlie Levitzky, Fassett Family Collection
Page 82: Trio, by J.R. Eyerman/*Time & Life* Pictures/Getty Images
Page 93: Spring flowers, by Jeff Norman
Page 94: Rancho Sierra Mar Restaurant, both photos by J. W. Post III
Page 116: Hopkins family, by J.R. Eyerman/*Time & Life* Pictures/Getty Images
All remaining photos, Hopkins Family Collection

Artwork credits:
Page 10: *View of Big Sur Coast*, oil, 1986, by George Choley
Page 156: *Portrait of Nan*, oil, 1989, by Sheila Healey
Page 159: *Horse and Rider on Partington*, oil, 1989, by George Choley

Library of Congress Cataloging-in-Publication Data
These Are My Flowers: Raising a Family on the Big Sur Coast—Letters of Nancy Hopkins
Edited by Heidi Hopkins
ISBN 978-0-9702294-3-4

Manufactured in China
Designed by Linda Herman, Glyph Publishing Arts
First Edition 2007

In memory of Nan and Sam,
with gratitude

Acknowledgments

In compiling this book, I had help from Jeff Norman, Bette Somerville, Ted and Marty Hartman, Linda Grant, Rosita Lopez, Tootie Trotter, Sylvia Trotter Anderson, Stephen Jory, Lloyd Bary, Gwynneth Carothers, and my brother, Craig. I also availed myself of resources in the Big Sur Historical Society archives and books by Jeff Norman, Gui de Angulo, Nicholas Roosevelt, and Henry Miller. Friends Eric Hansen and Susan DesBaillets offered excellent suggestions on an early draft; Jerry Sprout helped solve a problem late in the process; and Becky Soglin and Judith Goodman provided wonderful editorial guidance and encouragement all along the way. I am most grateful for this help.

My husband, Jim Merz, with his excellent computer skills, provided sorely needed technical support. And my sister, Darien Raistrick, with her astounding memory, artistic sensibilities and uncanny ability to find things, helped in uncountable ways.

Most of the photos used in the book are from our family collection. To fill in gaps, I had help from Jeff Norman, Erin Gafill, Soaring Starkey and the Post family. My nephew, Simon Raistrick, photographed Nan and Sam's letters. Finally, my brother-in-law, Ian Raistrick, was helpful in many, many ways…scanning and improving images, photographing artwork, and most importantly knowing our family photo collection backwards and forwards. Thank you.

George Choley, for many years a resident on Partington Ridge, painted the coast view from Partington (page 10) and the horse and rider (ridge neighbor Mary Lu Torén) (page 159). Portraitist Sheila Healey, our next-door neighbor for many years and a great friend of my mother, painted the portrait of my mother (page 156). Their art speaks volumes.

Contents

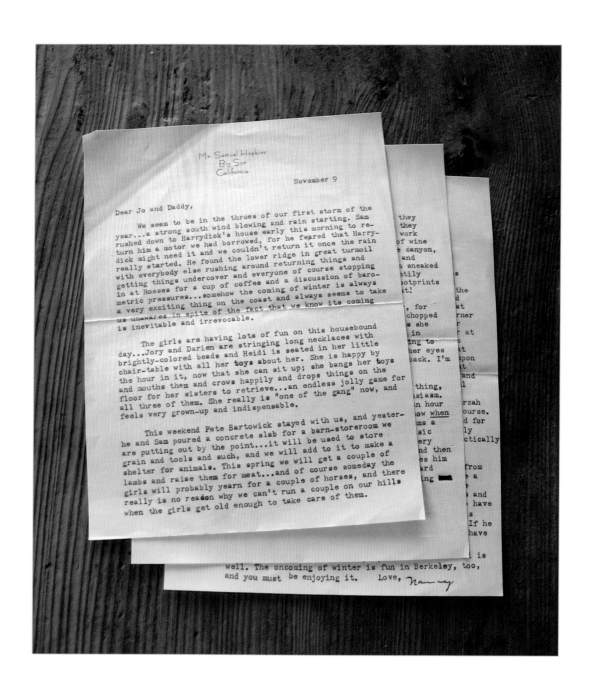

Mr. Samuel Hopkins
Big Sur
California

November 9

Dear Jo and Daddy,

We seem to be in the throes of our first storm of the year...a strong south wind blowing and rain starting. Sam rushed down to Harrydick's house early this morning to return him a motor we had borrowed, for he feared that Harrydick might need it and we couldn't return it once the rain really started. He found the lower ridge in great turmoil with everybody else rushing around returning things and getting things undercover and everyone of course stopping in at Rosses for a cup of coffee and a discussion of baro- metric pressures...somehow the coming of winter is always a very exciting thing on the coast and always seems to take us unawares in spite of the fact that we know its coming is inevitable and irrevocable.

The girls are having lots of fun on this housebound day...Jory and Darien are stringing long necklaces with brightly-colored beads and Heidi is seated in her little chair-table with all her toys about her. She is happy by the hour in it, now that she can sit up; she bangs her toys and mouths them and crows happily and drops things on the floor for her sisters to retrieve...an endless jolly game for all three of them. She really is "one of the gang" now, and feels very grown-up and indispensable.

This weekend Pete Bartowick stayed with us, and yester- he and Sam poured a concrete slab for a barn-storeroom we are putting out by the point...it will be used to store grain and tools and such, and we will add to it to make a shelter for animals. This spring we will get a couple of lambs and raise them for meat...and of course someday the girls will probably yearn for a couple of horses, and there really is no reason why we can't run a couple on our hills when the girls get old enough to take care of them.

well. The oncoming of winter is fun in Berkeley, too, and you must be enjoying it.   Love, Nancy

Preface

Nearly a year after my mother died, I spent time emptying her bureau drawers and cleaning out her closets. In one of many cardboard boxes, I discovered several shoeboxes filled with letters neatly stored in their faded envelopes, over 250 letters in all. These were letters from my mother in Big Sur to her parents in Berkeley; a few were from my father. The earliest postmarks dated from 1949, about a year after my mother had married, and the correspondence continued well into the mid-1960s. Most of the letters were two or more pages long, densely typed. They were begun during an era when phone lines had not yet reached Big Sur; they were my mother's means of sharing her life in Big Sur with her parents who lived 150 miles away.

Writing about what she loved most—her husband and children, her pleasures at home and with friends, the books she read, the nature that surrounded her—my mother captured a time and place in her characteristically positive prose. In terse counterpoint, my father penned a few letters over the years but more often used his annual rainfall record to note key events.

In compiling this narrative, I changed little of my mother's writing and simply made selections from her correspondence. In addition, I selected from my father's few letters and from his annual rainfall records, including only those entries that offer color or contrast to Nan's narrative. To round out the picture, I provided an introduction to the narrative, a bit of context for each chapter, and sidebars with background information about people mentioned by my parents.

In an attempt to keep this narrative compact and understandable to a reader not familiar with the people involved, I chose to limit the number of Big Sur residents who are mentioned by name. I focused on those neighbors and friends whom Nan mentions frequently in her letters over the course of the 14 years that make up this book. The result is that a number of our neighbors and of my parents' good friends are referred to as "a neighbor" or "a friend," including my father's hunting and fishing buddies; my mother's musical friends, the Grants; and our closest neighbor (after 1955) and one of Nan's warmest friends in later life, the artist Sheila Healey.

This compilation offers the reader one family's experience on the Big Sur coast in the 1950s. For me, it evokes a childhood that was as alive and richly textured as Big Sur itself.

Heidi Hopkins
Big Sur
May 2007

Introduction

B ig Sur in the 1950s was a quiet place. Since the late 1800s, the rugged geography of the Big Sur coast had attracted a diverse set of people sharing little other than a willingness to homestead and a desire to live off the beaten track. With the opening of Highway 1 in 1937, a wave of newcomers moved into the "rough land to the south," and new businesses opened. Despite this growth, the Big Sur community remained small, perhaps 300 residents along a 60-mile section of coast, and there was plenty of elbow-room. In the 1950s, residents were a mix of ranchers, highway workers, artists, bohemians, wealthy retirees, writers, motel owners, restaurateurs, and descendants of the Mexican Californians and the area's native people. They found ways to carve homesites—tucked almost invisibly away—out of the land's steep hillsides and lush canyons. These locals shared Highway 1 with tourists in the summer and had the coast to themselves for nine quiet months of the year. During these quiet months, you could drive to "town," 30 miles north on Highway 1, and not pass a single other car along the way.

The views along this stretch of California's coast are spectacular, but Big Sur—both then and now—is no easy place to live. The land rises steeply from the ocean to the Coast Ridge, which at 3,000 feet or more is high enough to catch and hold the weather. Storms slam into the land after a long Pacific reach and wreak havoc on roads, homes and electric lines. Summer brings dense dripping fog to the lower elevations, scorching heat up above, and an infuriating abundance of flies and other insects. Wildfire is an annual threat during the coast's long dry season, which typically stretches from June to late October. And the fundamental isolation of the area, inspiring in small doses, can weigh heavily when winter rains drag on, when the power is out for days or when a slide along the highway closes off access to the outside world.

But the elements that make life hard on the coast also provide a wonderful opportunity for community. The people who persist through the hardships share a passion for the place. They love the heart-stopping beauty. They thrive on the intimate, vigorous, at times overwhelming give-and-take relationship with nature. They accept inconvenience as the price of freedom from society's conventions. And overall, particularly in the hard times, they embrace the diverse set of creative, stubborn, generous and quirky folks who call Big Sur home.

＊　＊　＊

Our family home described in this narrative sits high on Partington Ridge, some eight miles south of the Big Sur Valley. Partington Ridge spills in a long, curving staircase from 3,000 feet elevation in the Coast Ridge down to the crashing surf. Ponderosa pines cluster on knolls along the higher portions of the ridge, while oak, bay laurel, poison oak and madrone fill the draws. Tall redwoods rise out of the canyon depths alongside perennial spring-fed creeks. Above the wooded draws, wild lilac and dense, prickly chamise blanket the steep upper flanks of the ridge; grassy meadows grace the middle portion; and coastal scrub—sweetly scented with black sage— covers the lower 1,000 feet where in summer the fog hugs the land like a blanket.

Coast pioneers homesteaded portions of Partington Ridge in the late 1800s. By the 1920s, the homesteaders had sold their properties to linguist Jaime de Angulo and to a consortium of Christian Scientists (as well as assorted intellectuals), who in turn subdivided and sold the land to the wave of newcomers who came in after Highway 1 was completed in 1937. By 1947, a number of people were living on Partington Ridge and formed an eclectic coast neighborhood. In addition to my parents, these included Big Sur–born Frank and Walter Trotter; writer Henry Miller; sculptor Harry Dick Ross and his writer wife, Lillian Bos Ross; retired diplomat Nicholas Roosevelt and his wife, Tirzah; sculptor David Tolerton and his wife, Bettina; anthropologist Maud Oakes; general contractor George Whitcomb; second-home owner Dryden Phelps, a doctor of divinity from Berkeley; and a year or so later, mosaicist Louisa Jenkins. In succeeding years, others purchased lots and built homes, home-building that has continued to the present.

＊　＊　＊

My father, Samuel Hopkins, was the great-grandnephew of Mark Hopkins, one of the "Big Four" who garnered federal subsidies and built the Union Pacific railroad across the country in the 1860s. Sam's grandfather, E.W. Hopkins, made his fortune on the shirttails of his uncle Mark's railroad success, developing the first refrigerated rail cars—using ice sawn out of Sierra lakes—to transport fresh produce east from the West's productive farm valleys. The wealth generated by E.W.'s enterprise flowed down to his children, and ultimately to his grandchildren, including Sam.

Sam was born in San Francisco in 1914, where he lived on Nob Hill with his father, also named Samuel, and his mother, Elyse Schultz Hopkins, the upwardly mobile daughter of German immigrants. At age seven, Sam was taken to live in New York City after his mother divorced his father in a bitter dispute. There he lived his mother's high life in a stately apartment with a butler and house servants; he attended prestigious St. George's prep school in Rhode Island; and he entered Yale, following the standard educational route of the day for the country's elite and fulfilling his mother's ambitions for her only son. Summers, they returned to California

Sam

and spent time both on the coast at Pebble Beach and at Emerald Bay on Lake Tahoe. Later in life, Sam described his blissful weeks at Lake Tahoe, where he and a friend filled the long hot days with boyish pranks and adventures. "I finally had a real boyhood," he recalled.

Samuel Sr. died when Sam was 12. When Sam turned 18, he assumed control of the family wealth. By age 20, he had dropped out of Yale, moved back to California and visited Big Sur for the first time. In a later letter he described his first impressions of Partington Ridge: "What a blaze of glory it was when I first rode a mule up Sam Trotter's trail and emerged from a high June fog to see yuccas in bloom. Pristine country with blue, blue skies and pines on the ridge. I couldn't believe it. There were bucks in the canyons and fish in the streams. From the highest ridge I could see the Sierra. What a place to be young!"

※ ※ ※

My mother, Nancy Jory, also descended from a family intimately linked to California's historical development. She was the great-granddaughter of John LeConte, who was invited out to California to help found the University of California along with his brother Joseph LeConte. These two men had had their careers dashed by the Civil War, which demolished the South

Nancy

they were born into and closed the door on Northern academic opportunities for Southerners. The relative wilds of California offered the academically minded brothers their best prospects after that terrible war.

Both LeContes settled in Berkeley. Both became professors, and Nancy's great-grandfather John served as president of the young university for a number of years. The LeConte descendants continued in Berkeley, where Nancy Jory was born in 1926.

Nancy's father, Arthur Jory, the son of Cornish immigrants, worked as an architect; her mother, Josephine LeConte, maintained the household and took in boarders to help make ends meet. The family income was modest, but it was enough to have food on the table during the Depression, and some to spare for more unfortunate people knocking on their door. Much of this food was grown in the family's extensive garden of vegetables, berries and fruit trees. Music was a family passion, and every family member, including Nancy's two brothers, played an instrument—whether piano, violin, viola or cello. (Nancy played both violin and viola.)

Nancy attended the University of California, Berkeley, and graduated with a degree in English literature, furthering her passion for the written word that began in earliest childhood despite her parents' complete lack of literary interest.

"Ever since my very early childhood I have been a lover of public libraries…so cool and silent…such a haven from everything that presses on the outside. I can still remember the happy winter afternoons I used to spend in the Berkeley library during my teens, afternoons which somehow imperceptibly slipped into winter evenings, for when I emerged, drugged, with my books under my arm the lights of downtown Berkeley would be on, and the mist would be damp against my face, and I would begin the climb up the hill to my home so freshened and exhilarated and exultant because life seemed so full of promise…."

* * *

My family's story on Partington Ridge began in 1939 when my father paid $3,000 for a 36-acre lot at the top of the subdivided area of Partington Ridge. He was 24 years old. At the time, there were only a few others living on Partington Ridge, among them linguist Jaime de Angulo.

My father used the property as a getaway place whenever he was tired of Carmel, where he had a home. He hauled in an eight-by-ten-foot construction shed and refurbished it as a permanent hunting camp for himself. His first "ground-breaking" was for a large, rectangular, spring-fed pool poised on the spine of the ridge. This pool preceded by many years any further construction…not only did Sam's service in World War II intervene but also the small cabin served Sam's basic, bachelor needs. The pool was Sam's respite from the baking heat of summer, the ridgetop itself was his palace, and the expansive views over steep, wooded canyons to the wrinkled Pacific below gave him his sense of home.

In 1947, Sam met Nancy on a Sierra Club High Sierra knapsack trip. Sam was 32; Nan 21. After Sam met Nan, everything changed for Sam. He set to work building a home suitable for

Neighbor Harry Dick Ross framing our house

Nan's parents, the "Jo and Daddy" to whom Nan's letters were written

his prospective wife. He hired his friend and neighbor Harry Dick Ross. Together, they constructed a simple, 20-by-40-foot rectangle with an open layout and beamed ceiling. The kitchen corner faced south and east over Partington Canyon and the south coast; the "bedroom" corner faced west, with a panoramic view over wooded Torre Canyon and out to sea; a large brick fireplace with a copper hood anchored the north wall, balanced by a plate-glass window across the room with views out to a massive interior live oak and the spring-fed pool. The rough-sawn redwood they used to build and panel the house had been milled at Big Creek a few miles south—the cost was $58 per 1,000 board feet, as my father always liked to remind us.

One of the final touches Sam made to the simple home was the dining table. With the countdown of days to the wedding, Sam and Harry Dick threw together a four-plank, eight-foot-long redwood dining table, rather like a picnic table, and set it on spare chimney stacks. They built two sturdy redwood benches to match. Harry Dick, ever the sculptor, decorated the table ends with chiseled fluting. This table was to be used until Sam could build a "proper" table. The "picnic" table is still in place with the patina of 60 years of nicks and stains and children's crayon doodles—still very much the heart of the home. Many of the letters that make up this narrative were tapped out by Nan on a typewriter as she sat at this table on rainy evenings, the children tucked into bed and Sam reading quietly by the fire.

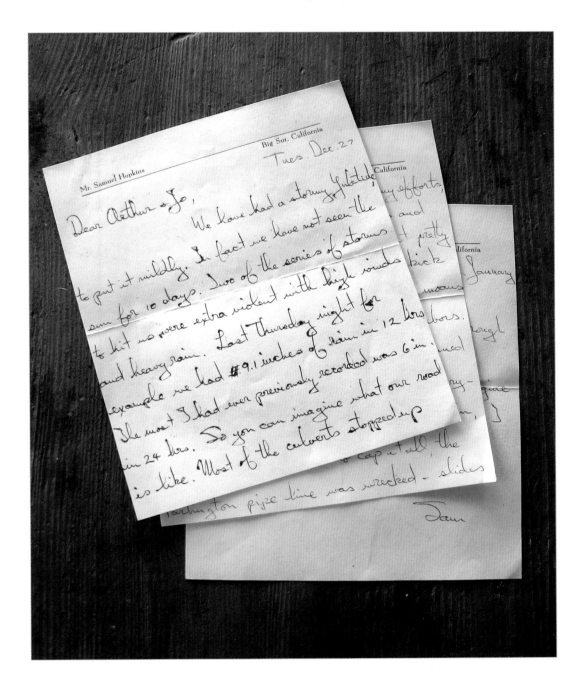

One

"I think everyone should marry young..."

Nan was 22 years old in August 1948 when she married Sam and moved to the Big Sur coast to live in their newly built home. She left behind her gregarious life in the city — a job at the *San Francisco Chronicle*, Berkeley's libraries and bookstores and intellectual stimulation, regular musical gatherings in the family home. She brought with her an extensive library, books gathered since earliest childhood, and merged it with Sam's fine collection, filling the floor-to-ceiling bookcases that lined the walls of their new home. These books, her new husband and the vast expanse of nature that dropped away from the house perched on the ridge were the mainstays of her happiness in the year and a half before her first child was born.

Nan's letters to her parents during this period describe a variety of local social events. Between these activities there would have been long stretches of solitude so quintessentially "Big Sur." If this solitude occasionally weighed on her, or if there were strains adjusting to her new husband, she never breathed a word of it. She was a woman of her generation, always finding that "there's a silver lining through each dark cloud shining." Nan never complained and rarely did she mention the darker moments of her life. Whatever troubles she may have had, they are left to our imaginations to ponder.

February 1949

I think everyone should marry young...that is, as soon as they're sure they've found the person they can't live without. You can really build a closer life together when you start young. And certainly the most wonderful period in your life begins with your marriage, so why put it off any longer than you absolutely have to? It astounds me when I hear of these long engagements or indefinite relationships such as "going together" that drift on for ages in a vague state of indecision. Such couples can't be in love in the real sense or they simply couldn't wait like that. And if they're not really "in love" they shouldn't marry at all, because in spite of all the sensible advice doled out by the many people who have never been in love as to the "sensible" reasons for marrying, I do feel that the final and most important reason for marrying is that you just cannot bear to live apart any longer.

We'll certainly wrap our children in a vast world of love, and I can't wish for anything better for them than the happiness we have. If parents love their children I should think they'd be eager

Jaime de Angulo

A brilliant and unconventional student of Native American languages, Jaime de Angulo was an early resident of Partington Ridge, acquiring a homestead patent around 1920 on a property spilling into Torre Canyon, on the west side of Partington

Ridge. Here he developed his ranch, Los Pesares, working the land and managing it as a small-scale dude ranch when he was not off conducting linguistic field research.

Jaime was a wild one. Born to Spanish expatriates in Paris, Jaime came to the United States at 18, and after a stint as a shepherd, he studied medicine and later linguistics, a career that brought him in contact with all the greats in the field…though not always with happy results. His wild and eccentric ways kept him outside the pale as far as conventional linguists were concerned. At Partington, Sam remembered Jaime riding naked on his horse and generally flinging convention to the wind. When Nan was introduced to him, before my parents married, Nan overheard Jaime telling my father that "she won't do."

Jaime must have appreciated my father though. In a 1947 letter, Jaime wrote: "He is a lovely boy. There he stays all by himself in his little cabin, reading Bertrand Russell or essays on poetry, or making trails in the woods, or hunting with bow-and-arrows...."

[Note: This letter was quoted in *The Old Coyote of Big Sur*, a book about Jaime's life by Jaime's daughter, Gui de Angulo. This is a fascinating book, well worth reading.]

Gathering with friends and neighbors

to have them marry and establish their homes. Sam and I have no "plans" for the children…and certainly no expectations. We just want them to love and be happy. There would be much less neurosis in this world if parents stopped expecting "great things" from their children. Anyway if they can be happy, isn't that a "great thing"?…probably the rarest thing.

October 1949

We're having a ridge fun-party next Wednesday at our home. Maud is going to show her color slides of the Guatemala interior where she spent several years studying the native cultures and Sam will show some of his best pictures of the Santa Lucias and the Sierra. Each family is contributing one part of the dinner and we'll have a buffet feast. Then on Halloween, there's going to be a costume party at Nepenthe, and everyone in the whole country will be there. How they love any excuse for a party down here!

November 1949

Isn't the coming of winter exciting? We love summer dearly, but there is something so warm and friendly and just-us-alone about the winter; fat orange madrone berries and bright red toyons and lovely grey wheeling flights of band-tailed pigeon. And then just the sunsets alone! And the delicious crashing storms that make our rafters groan and the pines outside bend and sigh.

Harry Dick Ross and Shanagolden

Harry Dick—sculptor, singer, lover, man-of-all-trades—first came to Big Sur in 1924, walking the coast trail from the south with his wife, Shanagolden (the writer Lillian Bos Ross). After years of barely making ends meet in various locations, they

were offered an opportunity to caretake a Big Sur property in the early 1930s, and in 1947 they managed to purchase their own property and build a small home on Partington Ridge.

While his passions were sculpting, playing guitar and singing with friends, Harry Dick earned his living as people do in Big Sur…any way he could. He tended bar at Nepenthe and hired himself out as a carpenter. He combined artistry with function, carving wooden business signs that set the standard for signs used along Highway 1 to this day.

Shanagolden tapped away at her typewriter, writing novels about early coast days. Her novel, *The Stranger*, set in late-1800s Big Sur, met with significant acclaim.

Fond of his "cigareets," Harry Dick had a thick, gravelly voice that blended nicely with a scotch and a strummed guitar. His laugh was strong and ready, as were his stocky body and blunt, capable hands. His daily toast was "to kindness."

During the rainy months our situation is unpredictable, for the road becomes impassable during storms…we try not to make any plans at all during the wet time and just hole in by ourselves. [Note: Nan frequently used ellipses in her writing. The ellipses that appear in the text of this book are hers and are not meant to indicate missing text.]

December 1949

Next Friday evening we shall attend the school Christmas play at the Grange Hall, which is the Big Event of the Big Sur social season. The kids put on a play which is always very bad and consequently great fun, what with the prompting and the homemade costumes and all the other accoutrements of school plays. Harry Dick is to be Santa Claus, and stockings will be given out to all the children down to the smallest baby and then there will be refreshments and great wassail and dancing for the oldsters. They really make an event out of it. Bill Post will play his accordion and others will bring their guitars and pocket flasks will be illegal but rife.

✳ ✳ ✳

We're in the midst of one of our "three-day blows" that move in from the south in such a methodical pattern…first an overcast day with a strong south wind that usually approaches gale proportions; then during the second day the ceiling slowly lowers and a light rain, blowing always from the south, commences; late the second day the rain settles into a downpour, straight down with no list from the south; gradually the list of the rain starts from the north on the third day, and becomes gentler, and a north wind starts, and the sky gradually clears of clouds and we are left with a bitterly cold clear fourth day.

February 1950

All sorts of things have happened down the coast…a whole mountainside of granite came down on the highway at Partington Point and the Roosevelts' light plant blew up and our road slid in a dozen different places below Trotter's and much has to be done before anything bigger than Jeeper can get through. We *really* were hit in the last big storm…we had 8.5 inches of rain as compared with Carmel's .8 inches so you can see that a storm down our way is a *storm*.

The big slide that closed the highway was all the more amazing because it came long after all the rain was over and forgotten. All of a sudden one night the whole mountain just slid and left the Tolertons perched above a granite cliff instead of above a sloping brushy hillside. The road crew has been dynamiting down there for days to try to clean the road. Fortunately it is just south of where our road starts up the ridge so our comings and goings aren't affected. And there is a wealth of granite for anyone who wants it…Sam is going to lay in a goodly supply.

Frank Trotter

Frank was one of four boys born to Big Sur pioneers Sam Trotter and Adelaide Pfeiffer. The "Trotter boys" were renowned on the coast for their size, strength and capacity for all kinds of work. Frank and his brother Walter married two sisters, Fern and Guelda Fenton. In the mid-1940s, both Frank and Walter, together with their respective families, lived on Partington Ridge. In the 1950s, they moved on to other locations in Big Sur.

Frank contributed most to the building of our home. He bulldozed the road up to Sam's top lot on Partington. Later, he and Walter laid cribbing—out of huge, hand-hewn redwood timbers—along the spine of the ridge where Sam proposed to build his home, broadening the narrow ridge back into a spacious garden area. Working together, the brothers put in the water pipeline between the spring in upper Partington Canyon and the house, surveying and bulldozing the road, constructing a cement catchment dam and spending three days wrestling nearly one mile of 4-inch army surplus steel pipe into place along the outside edge of the road—a sturdy and dependable, gravity-fed water system that has lasted over 50 years. Frank labored over the cement floor of our home. It took days to pour the 20-by-40-foot slab using a manual cement mixer; and the finishing lasted long into the night, with Frank on his knees with the screed, perfecting the surface under the lights of his Model A Ford.

Frank was an independent building contractor who gave freely of his time and inspired boundless admiration. One friend called him "the closest thing to a saint the rest of us will ever see," and my father agreed: "If anyone goes to heaven, Frank would."

Frank Trotter's home on Partington Ridge, built by his father, Sam Trotter

* * *

Sam dragged an old piece of sawn redwood out of the canyon below the old Partington house and is working on three end tables which he is making out of it. He had to saw it in three pieces and lug each one out on his back…but it is beautiful old wood and well dried, having been there for years. The top is sawn and has wonderful black saw marks on it which he'll leave there, and the bottom is hand-hewn and rounded. Sam just has to smooth and polish them and make legs for them.

* * *

We had dinner with the Trotters last night on our way in to town…Fern had baked seven loaves of bread and four huge apple pies…she bakes about that much every day. Gad! And I'm not exaggerating when I say that her pie pans are the size of a steering wheel. I've never seen so much food go down human gullets as goes down the Trotters'.

I'll never forget the first time Frank and Fern came to dinner…I was still a blushing bride of a hostess, having been married only a few weeks. I had baked a berry pie and plunked it down proudly in front of Frank for him to cut. He waited a moment and as nothing else was forthcoming he said "Is this all?" incredulously and I said "yes"…rather timidly at that point. "Oh," said Frank, "I thought we *each* got one of these." Frank loves to tease me…I'm always the butt of his jokes.

Fern is getting in the "baby" mood again and I'm sure that ere spring departs another one will be on the way. Sam says that she is just a "vast, elemental Force of Nature" and indeed it is no coincidence that all the Trotter children are born in December. Come April, Fern just has to kick over the traces and merge with the Life Force!

March 1950

The Rosses have gone down to Death Valley for a short vacation…I'm so glad they're taking a trip. This is the first one Harry Dick has taken since I've been living on the ridge. He and Shanagolden have a hard time making ends meet. But after they paid their income tax this March they felt they were enough ahead to splurge. So they piled their dogs and sleeping bags into Effie and headed for the desert.

Maud Oakes is leaving for Europe and points east at the end of April…her trip will include more research and she'll probably be gone for six months. We'll certainly miss her on the ridge, for she is a wonderful person. She'll travel alone for she says that that is the only way to have things "happen" to one.

* * *

We were thinking just the other day of how different everything would be for our neighbors down here if they were suddenly transplanted to the city. Everyone down here is Somebody, but in the city a fellow like Frank Trotter would be of no importance. And a person like Nick Roosevelt couldn't drive around in his blue jeans in a muddy jeep because his group in society would put pressure on him to conform with the upper-class neighborhood in which his income would let him live. We have such diverse types down here…from the very rich like Mr. Brown and those with independent incomes of varying extent to the artists and writers and intellectuals with no money at all but of cultural background and good education and on to the workers who have no education to speak of but who earn a good living and live up to every cent of it. Each one is important in the coast community…the half-Indian Posts are in a sense the "aristocracy" of Big Sur because they are the "oldest coast family," and we all listen with awe to old Joe Post telling the story of meeting a grizzly bear in Logwood Canyon back in the 1870s. But up in the city what prestige would the Posts have? What would Joe's yarns mean there?

Sam's mother, Elyse Hopkins

April 1950

Now that the baby is only about three weeks off everybody is getting apprehensive and starting to work on me, which gets me all confused. Mother wants me to stay in town and I want to stay down at Partington…the doctor tells me to stay where I'm happiest because it would be inconceivable that the child arrive in less than the hour and a half that it takes us to get to town. The women down the coast all drive in at the last minute. But now Sam is jumpy because various people have taken him aside and urged him to see that I stay in town, yet he wants me to be happy and he knows I don't want to miss spring down the coast. So we're all going around in circles….

[Note: When Nan refers to Mother, she is referring to Sam's mother, who lived in Carmel.]

Two

"I wouldn't trade this set-up for any other in the world."

Holding the small bundle of her firstborn child had to have been a moment of supreme joy for Nan. She had always wanted children—lots of them—and now, with the tiny fingers and unfocused eyes and groping mouth of the baby girl on her chest, she had embarked on fulfilling her dreams. Nan's euphoria comes across in her writing as does a new level of maturity. Life with a newborn in Big Sur in 1950 was easier than in the pioneer days but still challenging. There was no electricity, no telephone, no day care or close neighbors, and always the rigors of winter storms and summer heat and long stretches of solitude. One of Sam's highest compliments for Nan was that she could "take it." She did take it, and thrived.

April 1950

Goodness knows, I knew little enough about tiny babies when we carried Jory to Mother's house from the hospital (squalling most of the way) and plopped her in the basket. But in about two days I learned! I had to! There was no one else around who knew anything. I'll never forget the agony of the first bath—I determined to get it over with and plunked her in the basin. There was Jory bellowing her head off and squirming around like a wet eel and me trying to hold her head and wash her and keep her from sliding around…I was terror-stricken and shouted for Sam who was in the garage and didn't hear me so I "carried through" alone and finally emerged, wet as Jory, but victorious.

We stayed in town a week at the doctor's request…and it seemed the longest week of my life for I was so eager to get down the coast. Sam was wonderful and plunged right in, too. He knew how very much I wanted to get down to our own nest and he kept saying, "Monday we'll go…rain or shine." So Monday it *poured*. Sam took one look at my crestfallen face at the breakfast table and said "If we hurry I think we can make it before the road gets too slick." Oh, I loved him at that moment! We flew around and bundled Jory into the jeep and raced down here. What rain! Jeeper leaked and bounced and lurched and skidded, but Jory, like the grand little trooper she already is, didn't let out a peep. We plumped her in her basket and built a roaring fire and I danced around like a mad thing in my frenzy of joy. Home looked like heaven. The hills and canyons and new green oaks and blossoming madrones were just as I had pictured them during my stay at the hospital and in town. I've never been so happy in my life...and I've been walking on air ever since. There may be no washing machine and no cook here, but I wouldn't trade this set-up for any other in the world.

May 1950

Summer has moved in with its warmth even though it's only May...Sam has moved our furniture back out on the screen porch (we eat all our meals out there between May and October) and the swimming is magnificent and the garden beautiful and the yuccas about to burst out.

Our garden is producing well this year. We are eating our peas already, and everything else is coming along beautifully...potatoes, tomatoes, chard, spinach, squash, cantaloupe, corn, pole beans, bell peppers, eggplant, broccoli, cabbage, sprouts, carrots, beets, onions, leeks. And were going to have loads of berries this year. We planted about six grape vines down on the other side of the pool, and will keep them trimmed low...the grapes near the house I'm training up for an arbor. They're just shooting up.

* * *

We've been above the fog for a week now and are having the most magnificent sunrises and sunsets over the cottony, undulating sea, but this morning the fog climbed to our level and we are engulfed in it, with the madrone tree dripping on the roof and everything very winter-like.

June 1950

We have Jory's basket in the corner under the bookcases. She is used to any amount of noise, and none of it disturbs her...thank goodness, since we only have the one big room. We have no qualms about turning music on at any time or having neighbors in to dinner...I feed her before they arrive and no peep from her until at least 11:00 in spite of all wassail and laughter and guitar-strumming and clatter of dishes.

As you can imagine, our Brightest-and-Best keeps me running...and what time I have that isn't needed for feeding her and doing the laundry (by hand because no electricity!) and keeping up some semblance of cleanliness around the place and masterminding our Veritable Ranch of a garden and such routine as manages to consume time...the hours that are left over I'm anxious to spend reading or prowling the woods with Sam in search of wildflowers or perhaps just sitting looking at our glorious sunsets and discussing life as couples will or perhaps just sitting (darn it, why not?) thinking about nothing, but absorbing some vestige of serenity from the world of nature...which is perhaps the greatest gift one receives from living in the country.

Wildfire

Wildfire is an annual threat to the families along the coast. As in much of the West, the months-long dry season stretching generally from June to late October leaves Big Sur's grassland and chaparral tinder dry and vulnerable to unstoppable wildfires. The fire season generally is worst in the fall before winter rains begin, when the land is parched. Anxiety builds as the weeks go by without rain. The smell of smoke prompts panic. For those most at risk, depending on the location and vegetation surrounding a home, it is hard to be free of a constant niggling worry until the rains finally come and dampen the fuel.

July 1950

I was a widow last week because Sam was fighting the fire over near Arroyo Seco. The fire broke out shortly after we got down here so all the coast men went rushing out again. Frank and Walter had their "cat" and "dozer" up on the ridge here on the Indian Valley side of the fire, Billy Post and others were packing supplies in by mule train from Chew's Ridge, Harry Dick was manning the central radio post in Arroyo Seco, and Sam was "hot-spotting" with some Forest Service men and a bunch of convicts from the Soledad minimum security prison. They were flown in by helicopter to spots where fire had broken out…they worked right next to the fire with shovels and just slept in the ashes. Supplies were brought in to them by helicopter…also water,

Nicholas Roosevelt

Nicholas Roosevelt, a relative of the presidential Roosevelts, brought a high standard of culture to Partington Ridge. He and his wife, Tirzah, retired here in 1946, when Nick was 53. He left behind a rich professional career (following his graduation in history from Harvard) that included serving in the American Embassy in Paris, on the American mission to Spain in 1916–17, in the Philippines in 1930, as U.S. minister to Hungary from 1930 to 1933, and as a foreign correspondent and editorial writer for the *New York Times*. He gave up the pressures of his career in order to have time for reflection and writing.

"I am glad to have shaken the dust of New York off my feet and to be able to be in the Big Sur country, where people enjoy the art of living and have time to think," he wrote in 1953 in his book, *A Front Row Seat*.

Born into a musical family, Nick began cello lessons at age nine. Though he had put down his cello during his demanding career, he resumed playing when in Big Sur and was an enthusiastic member of the regular chamber music gatherings on Partington Ridge in the 1950s. It is said that even into his 80s Nick could play Bach solos for over two hours without once referring to a sheet of music.

because the streams were all dry in the burned area. Sam was absolutely unrecognizable when he returned because they couldn't use any of the water for cleaning up…it was so necessary for drinking…so they all just got black from the ash and cinders and after all those days you can imagine what he looked like!

Harry Dick became the hero of the fire fighters…he was manning the central radio, and every group of fire fighters had a "walkie-talkie" along with them to send information to the central office. One group of convicts was sent across country to Strawberry Valley and they arrived there at the end of the day all grimy and exhausted and things were all fouled up…the food that was supposed to have been dropped there by plane hadn't arrived, and there the poor devils were, miles from nowhere with no water and no food. They radioed their predicament to Harry Dick and said they didn't mind so much about the food and water but they did want cigarettes. So Harry Dick went to work on the Forest Service office at King City (by radio) and said that something would have to be done about those convicts and cigarettes must be sent right in. (Harry Dick is a heavy smoker himself so was all in sympathy with those convicts.) The fellow in King City said that he'd see if something could be done…he was rather casual about it and Harry Dick was getting rather mad and said that something had "damn well *better* be done about it…those fellows want cigarettes and they'd better get cigarettes." Then the man said that, well, he was going to attend a Forest Service meeting in San Francisco tomorrow and he'd see if some arrangement couldn't be made about cigarettes for the convicts. (And the convicts there in Strawberry parched and hungry and no blankets, etc.) So Harry Dick blew up. "Meeting in San Francisco…HELL!" he bellowed, "Either you get some cigarettes in to those men tonight or by _____ I'm going to leave this radio and walk in there with some myself!" They got their smokes that night.

Everyone was marvelous to me while Sam was away at the fire. All the neighbors were concerned about Sammy's two "girls" marooned "up there"…so they all came buzzing up. David Tolerton brought me a load of groceries from town…Nick Roosevelt brought me an armful of roses…Shanagolden came up every day to see that all was well (she was a widow too). And other people just dropped in…one afternoon was so funny because Shanagolden, Nick, David, two friends with Nick, and two other local fellows converged upon the Hopkins aerie at the same time, making it seem like a veritable Grand Central station. It was like a surprise party. Later Shanagolden said that it was lucky she appeared on the scene to chaperone me with my six men callers!

We do have wonderful neighbors on the ridge…I can't imagine how it just happened that the nicest and most interesting people in the coast country happened to settle on this one ridge.

August 1950

Jory is going like a little dynamo these days as always…we just can't keep up with her. She covers ground at sixty miles an hour by rolling over and over and by inching along on her tummy…and is she noisy! If I put her in her crib when she isn't ready to sleep she manages to have the whole thing torn to pieces in nothing flat with the bed pad and the blankets tossed to the four winds. Sam and I stand by in exhausted amazement and wonder how we produced such an atom-bomb.

October 1950

There was a big drama on the ridge last week, which resulted in a tragedy. It was storming all week and the road was pretty impassable. We didn't even try to get down…just stayed snug and made our food stretch. Izzie and Edith, who live in a little cabin on the neighboring Angulo property in Torre Canyon, were cut off too. None of us had seen Edith for months and didn't know she was pregnant…she's very shy, and they aren't married for some reason so I guess she was sensitive about facing people. But anyway she was over six months along and all of a sudden started having contractions. They couldn't get out with their car so her sister who has been staying with them ran all the way down the ridge to the Roosevelts who have a jeep. (This was about 10 o'clock at night.) Nick drove into Big Sur and phoned for a doctor…then he waited on the highway and drove the doctor up to Izzie's cabin through the storm. But by that time Izzie had delivered the baby, which was born alive. When the doctor got there he did what he could for Edith and then rushed to town with the baby, but it died just after he got to the hospital. We all felt terrible about it, but I think that under the circumstances everyone did what could be done. Even if Edith had been in a hospital the chance of a 6.5-month baby living would have been very slim. As a result of all that driving around in such a storm in an open jeep Nick came close to pneumonia.

January 1951

Jory goes everywhere with us…New Year's Eve we took her with us to a party at Nepenthe. The owners had invited just a big group of their friends (mostly the artistic fringe) and closed the restaurant to the public. So we had a roaring fire and a good dance floor and music and bacon and eggs at dawn. We bundled Jory into her wooly pajamas and a little cap and let her sleep all evening in the jeep. Then New Year's Day evening the Rosses gave a big buffet-dinner party and Jory went to that with us, along with a lot of other coast kids who slept in the back seats of cars.

Dancing at Nepenthe

[Letter from Sam]

As I sit here Nan is about to start on last night's dishes, and I'm going to help dry them. Don't think she usually leaves dishes overnight. It is only when we have company and the company stays late…you know how it is. Frank and Fern Trotter came for dinner and a good time was had by all. Fern and Nan talked of girlish things (babies, etc.) and Frank and I discussed tools, building, etc. (he is now working on a building for a man down here that is to cost $30,000 and be, in beams and interior surfaces, entirely hand hewn…and the boys know how to use a froe and an adze). We indulged Frank in his favorite hobby…eating. He consumed almost an entire leg of lamb, 2 quarts of milk and a jar of your peaches…aside from other items on the bill-of-fare. Nan made some delicious whole wheat bread and Frank loves to twit Nan so he asked her where she got the Swedish hard tack…but I notice he ate all of it.

It is actually raining out now. O joy. I feel justified in staying indoors now. There are so many things to be done around here that in fair weather I feel criminally lax if I am not working at something. I have so many projects going at once that I have a wide choice. I don't know if Nan told you about the baby's room…it is completed except for the painting…and will be a warm, well-insulated little room. One of its walls is the back of the fireplace. I believe we find out what we need by actually living here and adapting ourselves to matters of climate and convenience.

I have been cutting more wood than ever this winter. It is really lots of fun. I now deliver as far south as Livermore Ledge.

At this time of year we see endless flights of robins heading south. I don't know why they come so late but I suspect it is because of the toyons. The berries are more plentiful this year than ever. It is curious that the band-tailed pigeons won't touch them, yet the robins and varied thrushes live on nothing else while here. Of course cedar waxwings are plentiful and juncos are superabundant. Last week at low tide I went abalone hunting and brought Nan some of her favorite shellfish. We sliced and pounded and fried and had a couple of fine meals.

March 1951

Believe it or not, we've been snowbound for two days. It's a heavenly white world with snow flurries every hour or so and all the trees heavily laden. There are big patches of blue sky and great frothy clouds scudding from the north. The sea is grey and angry and a little coastal steamer is heading north close in to shore with great waves breaking over its bow.

Sam and a neighbor went skiing today…they walked up to the ridge where the snow must be really packed deep.

Skiing on the Coast Ridge

Kids waiting for the Easter egg hunt at Post's

We're having the most beautiful spring weather here…everything is sprouting and blossoming. Our grape vines on the porch are shooting up into a real arbor and the garden looks magnificent. Jory is even more magnificent than the garden. She is all tan and healthy from being out of doors all day long and her cheeks are so rosy and round.

Sam has been very busy…he finished the screen porch on the north side of the house and was in the midst of work on the kitchen sink board when something went wrong with the septic tank so he had to dig it out and fix it. He is the world's best repair man.

* * *

We took Jory to the annual Easter Egg Hunt at Post's yesterday and had a wonderful time. The affair is held in the pasture on the hill above Post's…they segregate the youngsters into approximate age groups so the toddlers search for eggs in a big clover-filled corral, the grade-school youngsters in the oak-filled valley and the kids above 11 or so all over the hills. There was a labeled basket hidden for each child beside myriad eggs, and it really was a colorful sight with swarms of youngsters everywhere and plenty of beer and ice cream and festivity for the whole coast. It, along with the school Christmas play, is the big event of the year socially. Sam stayed home because he thought only mothers and children would go. He was so disappointed when I came home and told him that everyone in the countryside was there, including all the roughest and toughest of his cronies!

August 1951

Izzie (who lives down below us at Jaime's) came rushing up the other night to say that Edith was having contractions (she is four months pregnant again) so Sam drove to Big Sur and phoned for a doctor…then waited on the highway for him and drove him up to Izzie's where he gave Edith a shot to quiet things down and help her hold the baby. He had never been down the coast before and was amazed by everything…especially to find Izzie and Edith living out-of-doors and cooking over an open fire. After he gave her the shot Izzie brewed them a pot of coffee over the fire and they sat around and chatted…later when Sam drove the doctor back down to his car on the highway he expressed amazement that a woman could ride over such rough roads and expect *not* to miscarry.

Sam and I had to chuckle over it later…we women are more rugged than they think. After all, Fern bounced up and down the road in her Model A Ford and produced four with nary a hitch…but then Fern couldn't *not* produce them. She once told me about how she tried to get rid of one of her children coming too soon on the heels of another by jumping off their high porch onto the ground below (about 12 feet). Nothing happened! Good old Fern! (That bit of folly was back when she was "very young.")

September 1951

Right now Jory is "helping" Sam, who is converting the garage into a tool-and-utility room. Jory holds the boards while he saws and helps hammer the nails in with her little hammer (when she hammers she just hits the wall a resounding whack) but she does feel that she is

Jory at her table

being extremely helpful and is indispensable to Daddy in completing the project at hand. I can watch her through the screen door and she is beautiful and ethereal like a Renoir child…naked as the day she was born, for in this warm September weather we have chosen the path of least resistance. Rather, Jory chose it…she loves to be naked.

She eats her meals all by herself now and the scene is always enchanting. Sam made a low table for her…heavy redwood and very highly polished…and she sits at it in her little chair in a very grown-up manner. At suppertime she has candles on the table to provide light…as she gets more dependable about grabbing things we'll put a little vase there with flowers, too. After all, gracious living begins in infancy! When I call her at mealtime she comes scampering in from outside and rushes right to the table, drawing up her little chair and getting herself all seated and ready. Sam can't resist taking flashbulb pictures of her at her meals…she looks just like a little princess.

October 1951

In the middle of last night it began to rain…and *hard*. We were astounded because yesterday was clear and warm and at bedtime the sky was filled with stars. Of course we had left everything out uncovered and Sam had to rush around in his pajamas with a flashlight throwing canvases over the chain saw and the cement and various other things. My laundry was all hung out too, and this morning I had to wring it out anew and string it from rafter to rafter…the living room looks like a baby factory.

* * *

The ridge was gladdened recently by the arrival home of Maud Oakes who has been on the Riviera recovering from a neck injury received in an auto accident in Peru (doesn't she get around?). She is full of delightful tales of her adventures…while in Europe she met both Jung and Schweitzer and was very impressed by both of them. She will recuperate here until April when she will go south to Peru again to continue her research there.

And we were saddened by the dispersal of Lepska Miller…she just up and left…where and with whom only Henry knows. She and Henry "divided" the youngsters, which I think is a crime…Lepska taking Tony and Henry keeping Val. Henry indulges Val too much and she will probably become a little monster without her mother around…Lepska, for all her failings, was an excellent mother. A man of over 60 is not the person to raise a six-year-old girl. Jory will miss Tony…he was closer to her age than any child around (3 years) and they enjoyed each other immensely. He was a delight…all boy and sheer animal spirits and hair as white as his father's. Shanagolden always said that Tony was "pure light"…Sam called him "not a child as much as a Vital Force"…both phrases described him completely.

Henry Miller

The well-known author Henry Miller first stayed in Big Sur in 1944 and, with his books finally generating a reasonable income, was able to buy a house on Partington Ridge in early 1947, where he moved with his wife, Lepska, and his two-year-old daughter, Valentine. His son Tony was born in 1948. During the 15 years that Henry lived on Partington Ridge, he wrote voluminously, publishing roughly a book a year, and spent months at a time traveling abroad. He also changed wives, divorcing Lepska and marrying (and later divorcing) Eve McClure.

Henry moved in different social circles from my parents. His friends and cohorts were the bohemian writers and artists who gravitated to the unconventionality of Big Sur and to Henry's sphere of influence. He frequented Nepenthe's lively bar. In contrast, my parents preferred a quiet lifestyle, away from the clash of egos inevitable in the gathering of bright, creative and individualist folks around a good bottle of booze.

The truth is Nan found Henry discomfiting. She disapproved of his marital life, with its succession of women. She viewed Miller's literary exuberance as undisciplined, his subject matter as prurient. Her opinion of Henry was typical for the time. Henry's *Tropic of Cancer* and *Tropic of Capricorn*, generally viewed in the United States as pornographic, had been banned from publication in the in the United States after these books were published in France in the 1930s; it wasn't until 1962, at the point when Henry had moved south to Pacific Palisades, that these books were finally published here.

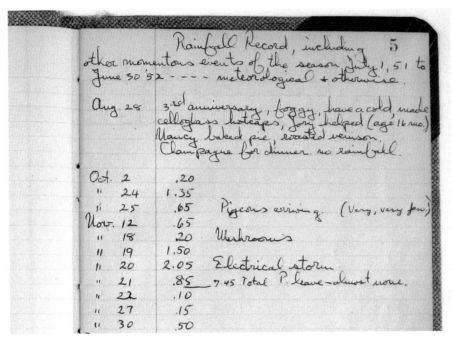

Sam's rainfall record

[Sam's rainfall record]

Aug. 28		3rd anniversary, foggy, have a cold, made celloglass hotcaps, Jory helped (age 16 mos.) Nancy baked pie, roasted venison. Champagne for dinner. No rainfall.
Oct. 24	1.35"	
Oct. 25	.65"	Pigeons arriving.
Nov. 18	.20"	Mushrooms

November 1951

Sunday was Val Miller's sixth birthday party, and it was a most roaring success. Henry had been going around in circles trying to plan the thing, with Shanagolden listing all the things he needed such as prizes and favors and colored hats, and Maud planning to bake the cake. There were 19 or 20 children there, ranging from 14 down to 8 months, and even more adults, and the Miller ménage was really a delightful madhouse. Such games and popping of favors and exploding of balloons and prizes and more prizes and ice cream for the children and wine flowing like water for the grown-ups. Maud had made the most beautiful birthday cake with real little wooden horses prancing around the top on a carousel that spun around under a striped canopy. Jory got away with a fantastic amount of ice cream and cake…everyone kept feeding her. But she has a cast-iron stomach and had no evil effects. We finally carried Jory home about six o'clock and plopped her right in to bed minus her supper…I felt that oatmeal on top of about seven pieces of cake would be a superfluity, to put it mildly…and such was her fatigue that she slept until 9 o'clock the next morning!

*　*　*

Driving into town last week I ran into Frank Trotter at the Bixby Creek Bridge and of course stopped to chat…we haven't seen Frank and Fern for months. Their new house up on Chapman's ranch is all finished now. Frank says that it is the first house they've ever lived in that doesn't leak, so they are very happy. Fern has acquired two more children. Stanley Dani's wife left him some months ago and he finally persuaded Fern to take the two small children left with him. So now Fern has six until Stanley gets a new wife or something. But she is indomitable in the face of chaos…Sandra and Richard are in school so she only has four during the day, but those four wet both their beds and their pants.

But an angel has dropped into Fern's life, as always. Just when things looked blackest someone miraculously appears to shoulder the load (and what could be blacker than Fern pregnant with six children?). This time it is an old lady of 70 who lives two miles from the Trotters. Every morning she walks to their house, does all the washing and ironing and most of the cooking, gets her meals as pay, and at night walks back up the hill in the dark to her cabin, unless Fern and Frank want to go out, in which case she stays with the youngsters until they return. Can you imagine a more providential angel? How does Fern do it? How do these people drop into her life and slave feverishly for her for absolutely no compensation? I feel that the answer is that Fern somehow *expects* these things to happen and so they do. Naturally, they would never happen to me or to anyone else because we cannot possibly conceive of their happening, let alone expect them.

*　*　*

I have a lulu of a case of poison oak. Last week when the men on the ridge spent the afternoon brush-cutting along the road Sam was deputed to work in the poison-oak because he doesn't get it at all. Sam can root it out with his hands and get the oil really rubbed in to him and he never gets as much as a tiny itch. When he arrived home at dinner time I was glad to see him and rushed with many a hug and kiss and lo and behold, the next day I began to itch and ere long it was all over my arms and back and stomach. I haven't had so much for a long time…but it was a lovely way to get it.

Trotter cousins from left: Sam, Richard, Sandra

* * *

It is bedtime now and it is raining…the sound on the roof is wonderful. Last night we had the biggest electrical storm we've ever had here…the lightning lit up the coast and the thunder claps were tremendous and very close. The rain came down in buckets and the wind was something terrific. Jory didn't wake up once, she's such a country mouse. You must have had the same storm in Berkeley, but somehow in the country storms seem more spectacular, perhaps because you have the sense of isolation and aloneness.

I love winter best of all…I get so joyful when a storm begins to move in that Sam always has to laugh. I'm so happy that this next baby will be a winter child.

December 1951

As soon as the rain stops for a while I put on Jory's rubber boots and bundle her up so that she can trot down the road after Sam to "help" repair any drains that are plugged. Yesterday the rain came down all morning in simply unbelievable torrents and Sam spent several hours working on the bad spot in the road just above Trotter's where the water always starts rushing down gopher holes and under the road, which can undermine it terrifically if the holes aren't immediately discovered and filled. The butane man is due to come up this month and we don't want him to be unable to get his truck up the hill…we're getting low on butane! If December stays this rainy we'll be cooking in the fireplace, but that's nothing unusual on the coast here. However, such amenities as hot showers are very welcome at times!

* * *

Believe it or not, we haven't been off the mountain for two weeks now…Sam has walked down to the Rosses, etc., but I haven't been off our land. People have been up here so we haven't been cut off completely from the world, but during the rain no car except a jeep can get up anyway so we don't expect to see anyone. The way we manage to stay so long without provisions is (1) pigeons, (2) quail, and (3) powdered milk. The milk problem we had unsolved for a long time. Sam and I drink lots of it…Jory still prefers the canned…but try as we will we can't keep it fresh more than a week. Then we discovered the new kind of powdered milk. You just shake it in a jar with lukewarm water and then put it in the icebox to cool…and presto, good milk to drink whenever you want it. Thank goodness we discovered it before we started buying milk for a brood of children!

* * *

Men are so funny about childbirth…childless men, that is, and even a few of those with children. They think of it as some mysterious ordeal, whereas in reality it is very simple and nothing at all to get worked up about. Harry Dick is the only childless man around here who is *not* that way. If I were to find myself alone with him at the crucial moment I would have utter confidence in his capability and good sense. Whereas I would have *no* confidence in Shanagolden, though I love her as much as I love him, for she always faints in any sort of a crisis. It is a coast joke. When anything happens in which Shanagolden should rise to the occasion, such as some injury to someone…even when Hotpot has puppies, she ALWAYS faints. Then everyone has to tend to her as well as to the original casualty. If Harry Dick cuts his finger or anything he has to be sure to put out an arm to catch Shanagolden as she crumples!

Nan reading by the fire

* * *

The Metropolitan Opera is broadcast on the radio now on Saturdays from 11:00 on, and it is magnificent. You must listen…we have followed it for three winters now and every year when November rolls around we can hardly wait for it to start. It makes us feel as though we are really familiar with the Met…I can hardly wait until we take a trip to New York some winter (between babies) and see some operas "in the flesh."

* * *

Somehow when I get through doing the things I have to do I manage to postpone doing the things I *ought* to do so that I can sneak in some time reading. I am in the Proust mood again and enjoying it tremendously. It's just as well, however, that I ration my Proust-reading to pregnancies or otherwise I'd never leave him for other authors. And too much Proust could conceivably be a bad thing. Sam balances my decadence very well, for he is in the thick of Sandburg's five-volume biography of Lincoln and is really making a study of the Civil War period. He talks about it so much with me that I feel as if I were reading it with him…likewise Sam and Proust. Our evenings are truly comical…both of us are so enthusiastic about what we are studying that we keep discussing our reading with each other and interrupting each other until Chase's political ambitions seem somehow inextricably involved with salon life in the Faubourg St. Germain.

* * *

We went down for the annual school Christmas play the other night and it was completely charming. The music teacher had planned the program in the form of the little tableaus to portray several of the most beautiful but least known traditional carols. The costumes were lovely and the children themselves completely delightful. Two of the older ones played recorders and all the children sang while they acted out the scenes (there are about 25 in all in the school). Everyone for miles around was there…plus all the babies and small children not yet in school. Afterwards there was a Santa Claus and presents for the children.

I love living in this community! Though I see (and everyone writes me to remind me) that it is now known as Utopia. That magazine article left a sour taste in my mouth, mostly because the woman who wrote it is a nervy little thing with a sugary smile and a will of iron. She invaded the Big Sur, determined to do an article on it, and at the end of her stay here all of us were glad to see her go. Last seen she was on her way to Ireland to "do" an article on the Emerald Isle. The article was interesting to me for one reason: it showed how a writer can take actual facts and write them up truthfully and yet somehow in the process of amalgamation the total picture takes on an entirely different aspect from reality. It is just enough colored by what the writer *wants* to think (or what she thinks the editor and reading public want to read) that she is not being true to things as they are. And yet being untrue without actually changing the facts.

* * *

The more you observe different personalities the more you realize that each individual is useful and happy if he is allowed to develop within his own framework with as little pressure as possible from the outside. The endless variations of personality are, almost without exception, worthy, and what is right for one is seldom right for another.

A wide knowledge of life is, to my mind, the best possible thing. I hope that by the time our children reach college age they'll have encountered a vast range of experience. Certainly a community like this one is an ideal spot for wide range of experience, for the class gradations go from the very rich to the very poor, from the intellectual to the physical, from the cosmopolitan to the insular. And there are few enough people that one can know and mix with them all.

* * *

I used to think that marriage didn't solve problems, but now I'm beginning to think that after all, perhaps it does. It seems to integrate your life and give it purpose. The reason I have come to believe that marriage solves difficulties is simply that *all* my married friends seem happy and constructive and outgoing…they write to us of things other than themselves…their children, their ideas, their simple pleasures, their plans for the future…the light side of life. While the unmarried ones, almost universally (and this is women as well as men), write great gloomy tomes of despair and torments and Monumental Woes…all connected with themselves. So I say Up with Marriage!!! Hurrah for the Tie that Binds!!! Away from the matrix of self and into the vortex of matrimony, where the only problems are "little ones," as Sam loves to say.

Three

"Child-raising is endlessly fascinating."

About a year after the second child was born, the electric line (but not the phone line) finally reached Partington Ridge. This enabled Nan and Sam to enjoy the major conveniences that had long been routine in urban areas—electric lights, washing machine, and freezer. (Prior to this time, they had a small generator to run a few lights as well as a propane refrigerator and water heater.) These new conveniences helped Nan find time to get back into the music that had formed such an important part of her youth in Berkeley.

Among the diverse people she encountered in Big Sur were several who shared her deep love for classical music and who had various degrees of training in chamber instruments: Brooks Clement, Emile Norman, Nick Roosevelt, Gene Perrine and Charlie Levitzky. It was during these next years that Nan took up her violin and viola again, despite having two small children on her hands. It is tempting to think that Nan's regained enthusiasm and diligence with music left its imprint particularly on her second child, Darien, who developed a fine, light touch on the piano as a young girl and grew up to teach piano to children.

Nan's letters up to this point had been handwritten. Just two months before her second child was born, Sam presented Nan with a manual typewriter. This became her faithful companion for the next 20 years.

[Sam's rainfall record]

Jan. 11	2.65"	*Lafler Canyon washed out.*
Jan. 12	1.40"	*All damage (slides, washouts, etc.) caused by 2 hr. downpour at midnight Jan. 11. It's not how much it rains but how fast.*
Jan. 13	1.00"	*Springs highest ever. Earth saturated.*
Jan. 14	2.55"	
Jan. 15	2.30"	*Cal. flooded. We move to town by doctor's orders.*
Jan. 16	1.30"	
Jan. 18	.35"	
Jan. 21	5.65"	*Two-day period—been in Carmel.*
Feb. 2	1.25"	*Darien born 1-28-52*

February 1952

Darien always has the most tender, sweet fragrance of graham cracker clinging about her. Harry Dick said to her the other day as he was rocking her in his arms, "You old sweet baby…your mother didn't born you…you just popped out of a graham cracker box!"

She couldn't be easier to take care of. She is gaining weight and we hardly even know she is around. We cuddle her a lot and get her out on the pouf to kick and be admired by the family. Jory wants to be forever kissing her, and is constantly amazed by her tiny hands and ears and her soft hair, which she strokes *very* gently! It is wonderful for Jory that Darien takes so little of my attention, for whatever misgivings she may have had at first about the new arrival seem to have been completely quelled.

March 1952

March is indeed coming in like a lion today…we have had snow all day since about six o'clock this morning. It is beautiful…the branches are tipped with white and the snowflakes drift down so silently. Occasionally a gust of wind comes up and the flakes whirl across the ridge-back from north to south.

* * *

Jory is getting very grown-up now at nearly three. She's good friends with Frosty, the dog that belongs to the woman helping us. The only problem is that the dog loves to wander and Jory trails after her. The other day I let Jory outside after her nap and went out myself just a few minutes later to check on her whereabouts and found her gone with the wind. I called and called, but no response and I could find no trace of her. So it occurred to me to call Frosty. Finally the dog came bounding down the hill, so I headed up in that direction to locate Jory. I was walking rapidly up the trail when I heard a little humming sound and there below me in the woods was the little scamp, marching back toward home (she hadn't seen me through the trees) with her arms folded on her chest, her hands tucked in her armpits, singing a tuneless little song. She is an independent little villain! She'll know this country like a book by the time she is six or so.

* * *

[Sam's rainfall record]

Mar. 14	*Cold south storm — hurricane velocity. Barometer lowest ever 29.30.*
Mar. 15 3.45"	*Higher winds! Will the roofs hold? 29.64 (Rocks on roof. Crawled.)*

Nan reading to Jory

* * *

Praise be for a day that, if very soggy underfoot, is at least not rainy or snowy or hail-y. Jory is out of doors…she has been cooped indoors for the last week or two and home has assumed many of the characteristics of Bedlam, with me the nuttiest of the nuts. All day long it has been "ree, ree, ree" and then "ree more, ree more, ree more." All this plus trying to get anything at all done such as meals or laundry or some semblance of housecleaning…and Darien, of course. The sight of Nancy Nursing Baby while at the same time trying to read to Jory and flinching as she hears the laundry boiling over on the stove and smells something burning in the oven is a tender domestic sight and not without its comic aspects!

I have been wondering how you people weathered the "big blow" two days ago. We have been having almost continuous snow since I got home from Carmel, and when it isn't snowing it is raining. To date we have had almost sixty inches of rain, and that is *some* record! We fortunately had no damage in the big wind, except trees down across the road. Fortunately, too, we had no trees down over our pipeline, for they might have broken the pipe.

We have two real little mountain girls…all through the big blow they were totally unconcerned.

Sam was very worried about the roof on our new little guest cabin, for the tarpaper almost ripped off, but he loaded it down with huge rocks and that way it held. If the paper had torn off the roof would have leaked like a sieve and it would have ruined the walls and furniture inside. There was lots of damage done around here…in one house down on the highway all the south-facing windows blew in and all along the highway there are tremendous slides. Several roofs lost their tarpaper with consequent damage to the interiors, and a neighbor had a slide on his hillside that has left his garage teetering on the edge of an overhang. I don't know how he can do anything about that except tear down the garage and bulldoze further back into the hill before he builds it again. As is he cannot leave his car in it. Thank goodness we aren't perched on the edge of a cliff as so many people are down in this precipitous country.

But time to bed down Jory (this letter has been in the process of being written all afternoon with many an interruption). Sam and I are going to picnic by the fireplace tonight…we always get these wild ideas and never fail to indulge them…we shall roast wienies and have a bowl of French-fried onions on the side…also celery and a bottle of wine and marshmallows afterward and we shall feel like the two happiest nuts in the world.

April 1952

Tomorrow I am going down the coast to play sonatas with Charlie Levitzky. The Levitzkys are a very nice couple…originally from Los Angeles where Melissa was teaching dancing and Charlie was an accountant. They moved up here last year because they wanted to live in the country…they have no children and can manage to live on what Charlie makes during the summer months acting as accountant for the State Park and its Lodge. So they make hay all winter and have a very, very happy life for themselves. We are having music once a week now and it is grand fun. On Sunday another friend buzzed up to see us…he is a screenwriter who plays the violin. He had brought his fiddle and we played some duets that I have just acquired for violins alone.

Charlie Levitzky

* * *

Saturday night there is to be a coast potluck supper…great institutions down here. Everyone comes…all the family…and every woman brings some great dish. Afterwards there is great revelry. The social life down here is such fun, with such a medley of types…the artists and the old coast settlers and all the rest of the in-betweens and all of us here because we love the country and hence there is some sort of homogeneity to the group. I shall brew up a great bowl of green salad for the event, for it is easy to fix and to take and our garden has such a plethora of delicious lettuce that I need to use it up some way before the new crop comes up.

July 1952

Our home frequently assumes an air of classic confusion…yesterday really took the cake…it was late in the morning and I had some jars of berries processing on the stove…also a pot of minestrone in the making…Darien wailing in her room as she fought off her morning nap which was imminent…Jory spraying Dutch cleanser all over the kitchen with great glee…the living-room strewn with all my underwear (Jory had earlier gotten into my undie drawer and draped bras and panties all over the furniture and I hadn't as yet had the time to pick them up)…and in walks Nick Roosevelt with some very, very proper people from the East who were very Hahvahd…they took one horrified glance around the room and at me with berry juice to the elbows and at Jory with Dutch cleanser and mud from head to toe and gasped out a feeble "Chahming! Simply chahming!" and beat a hasty retreat. Ah, life! I swear I don't know why Nick ever comes up to see us anymore… I'm sure that Nick returned home thanking his stars that the patter of little feet had never graced the halls of his manor!

September 1952

The only way in which I am a good mother (curiously enough) is my complete relaxation at this point as to what the children do or what catastrophes occur. Today when I put Jory in bed for her nap she called me back as usual for various things…the toilet, the drink of water, the kiss for her dolls Georgie and Sistie. Finally I told her that I wouldn't come in again, so she had better go to sleep. A few minutes later I heard a dreadful wail, but I ignored it until it began to sound like a call of genuine distress…then I went into her room and found her choking and spitting blood. So I turned her upside down and thumped her back and a bloody thumbtack flew out of her mouth. I gave her a glass of water, tucked her into bed again, and told her that she was to go to sleep now…No More Nonsense…and marched out of the room. She *did* go to sleep this time, and later on I marveled that I hadn't gotten in a stew or rushed her to a doctor…somehow my sixth sense warns me when a thing is serious and when it is not. At least I won't get ulcers!

* * *

Jory and I are having lots of fun with crayon and finger paints now…she is getting old enough to start working at crafts, and it will be lots of fun for her this winter when she is house-bound during the storms. But I have to take quite a bit of time helping her to use the materials…most children acquire those skills in nursery school and their mothers don't have to bother. But there isn't any nursery school down here for Jory or Darien, and so I enjoy the challenge of guiding their first creative activity myself.

* * *

The last few days have been terrifically hot here…the sun is baking and intense and we don't go out in it at all. The children play in the shade, which is always cool and pleasant, and the house is lovely and cool, too. These are what Sam calls September's "dog days"…we always have a few weeks of them just before winter moves in…they are a mixture of great joy and great despair and great anticipation and great idleness. It is a fruitful time…we bring in baskets of plump, fragrant figs and cool, sweet grapes…Muscat and tokay and purple Concords and pale seedless Thompsons…and round, orange cantaloupes and huge scarlet strawberries. But we long for that first storm of winter, starting with a greyness in the western sky and then a southern wind, gentle at first but then changing to a steady roar in the pine trees, and then finally the blessed, blessed rain.

October 1952

On Halloween night there is the annual big party at Nepenthe, after which it closes until April 1. Everyone comes in costume and tries to be absolutely incognito. It is truly a wild and hilarious affair. Everybody is already wondering just what wild outfit Shanagolden is dreaming up…she goes to fantastic lengths to make people believe that she is *not* going to attend the party…disappears from sight for days before the party and people are informed that she is hospitalized in Spokane or caring for an invalid aunt in Tucson or dickering with publishers in New York City and postcards from these places pour in to all her friends, leading them always to believe that, by jingo!, Shanagolden is really *not* going to be at the Halloween party this year! And then she appears at the party in some completely disguising garb and everyone just shouts as she slinks unobtrusively in the door, "Shanagolden! So you got here after all!!!" And she is always so crushed, but never enough to keep her from trying the same sort of subterfuge next year. Now beside wondering what Shanagolden will wear, the countryside always wonders what story she will devise to make them think that she will not attend a party which in actuality she would rise from a death-bed to grace with her presence. She is wonderful!

Shanagolden at Nepenthe

November 1952

We had a grand day at the beach last week…we took the boat down to the cove at Sycamore Canyon (near the State Park) and joined friends there with their boat. But the surf was too rough so the men didn't go out…we just walked along the beach and gathered shells and driftwood. It was a wonderful day, and perhaps Jory enjoyed it most of all. That is a beautiful beach there…a long, curving cove completely hemmed in by mountains…you reach it by driving across the Brazil ranch in Sycamore Canyon, driving across their hayfields which follow the small river right to the cove. It is very isolated, of course, as it is practically private land. Later that same week Sam took a boat out from Chuck Fuller's little strip of beach and came back with a great load of red rock cod and flounder. We dispensed fish up and down the coast, and just wished that we had our freezer so we could have frozen some of it.

When electricity comes here and we have the freezer, I imagine that we will never have to buy any meat at all.

Sam has been felling trees for the P.G. and E.…there has to be a swath cut for the lines where they go through the woods. The men arrived on the ridge to cut them, and they just had a dinky little hand saw. Sam nearly died! So he said that he would fell the trees for them, and they could limb the trees with *their* saw. Then he wrote a letter to the landowner, Mr. Brown, and informed him that he could have the wood and pay Sam for his labor, or else Sam would sell the wood to people on the ridge and pay a stumpage fee. Sam's wheeling and dealings with Mr. Brown (who is the wheeling-and-dealing-est man I've ever met) had me in gales of laughter…we haven't yet heard from him, but I suspect that he is sweating it out to try to get the better of Wise Samuel!

* * *

A gale of hurricane velocity is raising our rafters today… also a terrific rain blowing horizontally across the ridgeback from the south. This is the kind of November storm that Sam likes to think (and quite correctly) separates the men from the boys. I thought that I had seen storms in Berkeley, but a good southern storm here in the mountains makes Berkeley's heaviest downpour seem like a mere drizzle! Certain city-dweller artists who arrive in Big Sur in midsummer and are so charmed by its natural beauty and congenial populace that they rent some small cabin for the coming year inevitably leave the country hastily after the first "big blow"…the pastoral life loses its charms for them when they discover that they have to nail down their roofing paper amid pelting rain and terrifying winds and shovel out slides and clear fallen trees and board up broken windows and go without such delights as butter and milk for a week at a time. But for those of us who stay on to face life it has great stimulation and excitement.

December 1952

We had a farewell dinner for Henry last night…he and Eve leave for Europe next Monday. The Rosses and Tolertons and Maud Oakes also graced our board, and I had made a huge venison meat loaf which was delicious (everyone said…better still, they showed it by all coming back for seconds and thirds). It was the first time that Henry and Eve had ever had venison, so they were properly amazed. Dear Henry brought a bottle of whiskey, and I had to think "how true to life" for whiskey costs six or seven dollars a bottle and yet it will always be the poorest person…the person least able to afford it…who will *always* show up at the party bearing such a gift for the host and hostess.

He was full of talk about Val and Tony…nothing so delights my heart as a person who really loves his children as Henry does…he will go into endless little details about the imaginative games that Val dreams up and can recite her letter word for word…how she writes to him "Dear Daddy, Last night we played trick or treat. Do you know what is trick or treat? Trick or treat is when you go to someone's house and say trick or treat and they give you something." The way

Henry tells this little episode makes it seem like something not quite of this world, but of a sweeter, finer world which is childhood. And, also very Henry-like, he described his horror when someone…some progressive-school teacher friend of his… approached him to purchase for Val a book on sex-instruction for six-and-seven-year-olds and this book had "all the scientific terms for EVERYTHING… no euphemisms…just SCIENTIFIC WORDS! I WAS APPALLED!! Teaching those words to *children*!!!" The rest of us had to chuckle gently, remembering that after all Henry has written books any paragraph of which would be enough to curl your hair, and yet he cannot bear the thought that his daughter should even be able to call the parts of the body by their correct names!

*   *   *

We were on the verge of thinking that we would have electricity for Christmas. They had almost completed a 3000' span across Torre Canyon when the wires broke and our hopes for electricity lay in a tangled copper coil in the bottom of that massive canyon. They have to start all over…shooting a rope across with a special Coast Guard rescue cannon then using that to pull over a larger rope, then finally easing over the copper wire, untangling it from the tops of redwoods, being sure not to kink it.

It was funny, though; we all enjoyed a good laugh at the P.G. and E. men who have been lapping up our beer for the last three years while assuring us that the line would eventually become a reality. They still think that the line will be completed this month (Torre or no Torre) and have invited all of Partington Ridge to a great party at the Roosevelt's home next Friday afternoon at which all the liquor will be supplied by the P.G. and E. engineers and everyone will be free to drink as much as he likes (or can). I think that all of the so-hospitable Partington hosts who have supplied drinks for the engineers for the last three years are going to rise to the occasion even if it means pouring some of the drinks into Tirzah's potted plants! They are going to make the P.G. and E. pay up for all that guzzling…and believe me, an engineer can really guzzle! As for me, I shall stay home from the party. Engineers are the dullest people in the world!

*   *   *

[letter from Sam]

Last week I had fun working for the P.G.&E. with the chain saw. They really kept me busy with a crew of men limbing and stacking while I did the bucking. It was worth it though at $4 an hour. But tomorrow I have to go to town to have the saw fixed…so you don't get rich doing that sort of work. Just as an example: last month I made $112.50 renting the cat, yet since then my time and trouble plus spare parts needed to put the tractor back in good shape has eaten up a good deal of the profit.

Emile Norman and Brooks Clement

Artist Emile Norman (right) moved to Big Sur in 1946 with his partner Brooks Clement. Born to a San Gabriel Valley ranching family, Emile discovered his passion for art by the time he was 11. Despite no encouragement from his family, he single-mindedly pursued his artistic dreams and built a successful career that included museum and gallery shows, private commissions, public art commissions and the gradual building and decorating of their home, which itself became a work of art. Amazingly prolific and inventive and energetic, Emile worked in a range of media—wood inlay sculpture, mosaics, silk screen prints, etchings and bronze. Clem managed the business side of Emile's art and played Bach beautifully on the huge pipe organ that Emile had shipped from Germany and installed in their home.

Clem and Emile (affectionately called Clemile by their friends, so inextricably were they linked in everyone's mind) found kindred spirits in my parents, with whom they shared a love for music and an enthusiasm for walking in Big Sur's rugged and glorious coastal hills. There was a period in the late 1950s when Clem and Emile were such regular visitors to our home, particularly for Thursday chamber music gatherings, that we children called them collectively "Mailbox" since they never failed to pick up the mail from our box on the highway. "Mommy, Mommy, Mailbox is here!!" we would shout when we heard their car approaching up the dusty road.

Clem died in 1973; Emile continues churning out his graceful designs at 89 years of age.

Emile Norman mosaic

February 1953

We have been taking the girls out on hikes and picnics with us…Sam carries Jory (except where the trail is fairly level) and I carry Darien. We have been having glorious outings, and I don't know why we didn't start doing it earlier…for some reason it didn't occur to me to carry the baby on my back, which is so silly when I carry a heavier pack in the mountains. On Darien's birthday we took a picnic lunch and birthday cake and drove up to Emile Norman's home for a surprise-picnic…we all had a wonderful feed, and afterward Emile and Clem and I played music…the two men play recorders, and we had such fun.

Tomorrow we are going on a picnic with the Rosses and shall wind up at the Trotters' home up on Bixby Creek. We haven't seen them since last spring, and I (and Shanagolden) are very eager to see Fern's newest, Judy Ann, who is nine months now. If you think we never do anything but go on picnics, just put it down to the fact that in Such A January As This Has Been how can one do anything else? When it rains or colds there will be time enough for the prosaicisms of life. Truly we get things done in between larks…all sorts of plantings and fence-buildings and prunings and bull-dozings (Sam has been making roads for two of our neighbors). And I do laundry once a day and cook three meals and care for the children and keep the house fairly clean and do a minimum of gardening…so if we still sandwich in time for picnics and for reading Flaubert you mustn't think we completely ignore the Grim Realities!

Well off to hardboil some eggs for the morrow! Since we shall be off betimes in the morning for this mad excursion with two kids, two dogs, and four crazy romantic adults I want to have as little as possible to do then…just getting the two girls cleaned up and properly attired and into the jeep seems to take quite some doing!

March 1953

March is just glorious…I have been flying at the garden, and really feel in the mood. I have decided that one must never work in the garden unless one is in the mood… My mind has been cleared of much rubbish lately and I have come to formulate a philosophy that I should have arrived at years ago: namely, that one should work hard when one feels bum anyway and loaf utterly and unrepentantly on days when one feels magnificent. So if I have been kept up most of the night by wailing children or am coming down with the flu or just feel at a miserable low point of morale then I scrub floors and wash windows and launder the children's blankets and weed and spade the flower beds and mend overalls and in general have a miserable day. And then (oh joy) when I wake up refreshed and full of vim and vigor and the joy of living I do nothing all day but read and listen to music and practice my fiddle and take a picnic with Sam and the children and look for wild iris and roses or maybe go to the beach and look for jade and driftwood…just anything that is completely and utterly loafing.

*   *   *

Sam took a load of wood down to a neighbor this morning and in return for it the neighbor came up this afternoon and helped us with all sorts of chores. Yesterday we took the chainsaw to a friend's home and Sam spent the day felling oaks in return for some pipe that our friend got for us (he is a plumber). Don't we have the barter system worked out splendidly? Everybody down here is always doing something for someone else, but money never changes hands. We just work off the debt some way…it is fun and friendlier that way.

*   *   *

Easter Sunday Emile and Clem came up to see us bearing a basket of beautiful Easter eggs…they had painted them themselves, and we picked out four of them (one for each of us) and then celebrated the occasion by libations. You'd be amazed what a delightful work of art an egg can be when decorated by an artist.

April 1953

This week Alvin Brazil brought his bulldozer up and flattened our point out beyond the swimming pool. We had fun pumping Alvin on his family tree; the Brazils are one of the old, old coast families. The Pfeiffers, the Danis, the Harlans, the Brazils, the Trotters are the descendents of the original families that ranched this area and have so completely intermarried that any member of one of the families is a member of all of the others.

There are so many feuds that go back several generations…usually over somebody's cattle that trespassed in someone else's grazing land or somebody's husband who fathered her sister's illegitimate child. It is a vigorous mythology, full of the strength and color that seems so

Emile with Easter eggs

peculiarly American and yet which is so completely overlooked by these magazine writers who write about the chic aspects of Big Sur for such magazines as *Town and Country* and *Holiday* and miss the real Big Sur which has genuine vitality. Such stories as the one about Roche Castro ambushing and murdering a man on the old county trail down on the ridge here (Jaime de Angulo was the only witness and he held it as a weapon over Roche's head for years) and Ali Boronda following travelers across his ranch (the old county trail went through it) with a gun barrel at their backs…and such things happened only thirty years or so ago and I have heard them from the mouths of people who were right there on the scene.

* * *

Great excitement here! The long-promised electric line has been established on Partington Ridge, and we have great plans for filling our new freezer.

* * *

Child-raising is endlessly fascinating. I have often thought that the emotional problems that sometimes beset the first child in a family must have their root in the fact that it is always the "first" child who interrupts the honeymoon, as it were. Of course the first one is very much wanted and certainly thrilling because no young couple believes that they can really have children until the first one is born; but the oldest child is the one of all the family who is always usurping little fragments of his parents' closeness: as he grows older he usurps more and more of their shared intimacy; what he takes over and what his parents relinquish is automatically passed on to the younger children, so they never have to fight the battle with the parents of what will or will not be given and consequently the parents' faint, submerged resentments against this loss of their selfish pleasure in one another are never directed against later children but always subconsciously against the eldest. Of course one doesn't want to recognize this baseness in oneself, but I think that it plays a very real part in family relationships; if we recognize it perhaps it will be less harmful.

July 1953

Two days ago while I was playing music with some friends down the coast Sam took the boat out from their cove and came back an hour or so later with four fat rockfish, and then yesterday we took a picnic to a local beach and he took the boat out again for a short spin and came back with four fat red cod. So our freezer is getting filled up, and we can really anticipate the time when we can live off the land completely. My evenings have been busy ones what with making jam and making and freezing pies from the loganberries…I freeze them unbaked. Really a freezer opens up great possibilities…when I make anything I just make a double quantity and put half aside for the freezer. Bread freezes marvelously, and I keep a supply of things like homemade rolls that can be warmed up easily for a company dinner.

* * *

Our peach tree is simply loaded with fruit, and I learned to my sorrow this morning that the coons are already after it…so out comes a trap again; the little wretches just *won't* learn to stay away! The fig tree has been producing well for a month and will produce well into September…it is a most satisfactory fruit, for what we can't eat dries readily and we can eat it later as dried figs. Also the grape vines are loaded…great succulent bunches! They are so beautiful as they ripen…blue Concords and fat Muscats and rosy Tokays and shimmery Thompson seedless.

* * *

You of the older generation are so exhausting! Mother is exactly the same way; the minute she arrives she starts moving furniture and washing windows and buzzing around and when she finally leaves a couple of days later Sam and I collapse in a chair and relish the wonderful feeling of just Doing Nothing. Doing Nothing is something that only the younger generation is geared for; our young friends are such marvelous lazy companions…they never dream of working on a visiting weekend…they just sit and dream and read and go for picnics and sit some more and are all in all such idyllic people to have around. There is so much work that one *has* to do that it seems a shame to do any on such an occasion as a holiday weekend. But I suppose it is such energy as Daddy's that has put the world where it is!

August 1953

Nick Roosevelt wants to take up the 'cello again. He plays very well; one day he saw my viola lying on the table and he put it down between his knees and played one of the Bach suites on it and played it very well.

* * *

Once my children learn to read by themselves I shall impress upon them that a day is wasted unless you spend at least an hour reading…and two hours of reading would be a minimum during vacation time. I'm not trying to inflict my interest on the girls. They could read anything that stimulated their imagination and their appreciation of things; it might be books about science or geography or biography or how to ride a horse or how to curl their hair. But I just insist that they read enough to do it easily and to increase their horizons…whatever they may wish those horizons to be.

September 1953

Great things are happening here in a musical way; our friends Clem and Emile who have been playing recorders with me for some months suddenly made up their minds that there is no future for them unless they sink their teeth into some real instruments…this all came about because they brought up a violinist one night who played violin-viola duets with me and when the boys went home they said to each other "We're just wasting our time…we've got to take up strings." They went ahead and lined up teachers and got music and a friend brought them two instruments, both amazingly good ones. The boys were so thrilled that they had to sit right down and work out some notes and play Then And There with another violinist.

* * *

The girls and I buzz around and hold down the fort while Sam is gone. Yesterday it rained and I rushed around with tarps and things and covered equipment that he had left out in the open such as the tractor and the chain saw…also sacks of chicken feed…all things which I haven't the strength to move under shelter. Also I had to get our foolish chickens in to the chicken house…the little wretches haven't yet learned to go in where it is dry! After dark they won't "herd" and I had to chase them and carry them in one at a time.

The girls are well and full of beans…Jory has made it her responsibility to inspect the mousetraps every day while Sam is away and inform me if there are any customers…today we had two! I can remove them from the traps now without a qualm, showing what a good country wife I have become.Yesterday we caught the cutest little mouse in the world: Darien! She was exploring around the wine cellar and made the mistake of picking up what looked like a most lovely, rattly little toy. Bang!! Oh, did she wail! And did she suck her injured little pinky when she was released!

October 1953

Our general weather pattern has changed subtly over the years so that fall, instead of being our hot, hazy, horrid time is now about our most beautiful season…such crystal-clear days and sharp shadows and heavenly moons and sunsets…honestly, from being my least favorite month October has turned into my favorite month. It is so absolutely golden and peaceful and bookish and redolent of something which I never can quite express.

* * *

A friend recently asked me what I do in the afternoon "when all your work is finished?" In the afternoons the children like to explore the woods and collect leaves and climb trees and ride our donkey and ride their tricycles down the road…but they want my company on all of these adventures, and in a way they really need it, for there are always little emergencies coming up…girls getting stuck up in trees and girls getting pinned under trikes and girls finding that their own chubby hands are not big enough to carry home all the pretty treasures they find in the woods. Well, that is exactly what I "do!"

November 1953

Our new moppet started kicking around last week, which completely took me by surprise. With the first two babies I was always counting the weeks and anticipating the first little flutter, but with this one I have been so busy that I never give it a thought and was completely astounded to suddenly feel that faint, faint little bump.

View south in the fall

Sam splitting madrone

* * *

Sam is fine, and has been cutting a lot of wood during these last weeks of fine weather. It is stacked all along the pipeline road and looks quite magnificent. This next week he goes down to Livermore Ledge to bulldoze a trail down the cliff to a hot spring. The cliff is very steep right there above the ocean, but I know he will be careful…the danger is not so much for himself as for the tractor.

Poetic Exchange on Firewood

[from Nick and Tirzah to Sam and
Nancy Hopkins]

With winter now not far away
We view our wood stack with dismay
So even though we know that we
Must help support P.G.&E.
We'd like to have three cords of oak
Or good hard wood that doesn't smoke.
Don't come next week. We'll be away.
But after that come any day.

[reply from Nancy]
We wept to list that piteous tale
Of shrunken pile, impending gale,
Of gelid limb and blood congealed,
Of cheerless grate and frosty field.
We sobbed to think our wood of yore
Was wont to make that chimney roar
While merry clink of cocktail glass
Made chilly winter evenings pass;
Yet now that hearth abandoned lies,
No more a joy to fair and wise.

But fear not, friends, for succor comes.
The upper ridge with chain saw hums.
Great stacks of fragrant, rosy oak
(We guarantee it will not smoke)
Will shortly grace thy manor grate
And sparks fly up at joyous rate.
So may ye once more praises sing
To Stalwart Sam, the lumber king.

I remain, though never fancy,
Always your devoted
     — Nancy

[reply from Nick and Tirzah]

Out hearts wing o'er the chimney tops
At thought of wood from Sammy Hop's.
Please tell your sawyer of our joy.
We're ready to cry: "Jeep, ahoy!"
And guard him from ferocious dogs
As he unloads his precious logs.

Come one, come all, and drink a toast
To Sam, best woodsman on the coast.

     — Nickantirzah,
    the wood-be wood burners

[regretful lines to Nick and Tirzah]

Oh, miserable we, alack,
And woe and welladay:
The things that must perforce be said
Are hard indeed to say.

Upon a time, two tiny babes,
Scarce out of swaddling clothes,
Fell weeping at their father's knee.
(Their plaint we now disclose):

"Oh father, father, hear our plea,
And do not, in thy greed,
Forget thy spouse and tender babes
Who stand so sore in need.
Thou sell'st thy wood to Maud and Nick,
To Harry Dick and David,
Nor reck'st that from the wintry blast
Thine own brood should be saved.
Thy coffers ring with golden coin
And mayhap thou get'st rich,
But mother to keep warm must deck
Herself like Lapland witch.
Our fingers small with chilblains smart;
Our cheeks grow wan and thin;
We wear our mittens out of door,
But must we wear them in?"

Their pleading eyes were raised to him
As knelt the lovely twain.
Their father clasped them to his breast
While down his tears did rain.

"Oh beauteous pair---oh fairest stars
On Partington's horizon,
No more shall piteous crystal drops
Thy woeful eyne bedizen,
Or tiny fingers sting with cold.
No more shall Hopkins lumber,

While sounds of Boreas frights the skies,
The alien hearth encumber.
Lo, here at home the blaze will make
Our rafters cheer and gay,
While tiny, rosy, laughing girls
Will by its brightness play."

Oh, Nick and Tirzah, worthy friends
And dear, if this seems cruel,
Remember that there still remains
Keith's mighty Plaza Fuel.

(L'envoi) So let us drink a toast to Keith
With hors d'oeuvre and with liquor,
And shed a tear that Hopkins woods
Cannot somehow be thicker.

[P.S. by Sam]

Now that you've read this threnody
As of a Milton at his prime
It's far from difficult to see
This is immortal rhyme.

How sad it is! How dolorous!
That such a poet should
Expend her rapt imaginings
Upon a cord of wood.

I feel that she should sing a round
Of nightingales, of tiny folk,
Of castles, dragons, maidens bound
But not of 2 ft. oak.

As for myself I must admit
To slothfulness or worse;
Inclining by the pool to sit
With drink and book of verse.

My head was filled with fancyings
Inspired by that book,
Of dryads and their sufferings
(Of Zeus and his stern mutterings)
Whene'er an oak was strook.
Chainsaw, maul and axe away!
Impiety is rife
I dare not fall another tree
For that will end my life.

[Chilly reply from Nick and Tirzah]

Oh Hopkinses, oh Hopkinses,
Up yonder on your knoll,
To whom all Partingtonians
For wood long paid a toll,
We'd hate to think of little tots
With chilblains on their toes,
And Sam's new fear of dryads dear
And Zeus's threatened blows.
But why this sudden note of gloom
And threat of broken oath,
When oaks that long since met their doom
Are saved and dried? Is sloth
A fit demur to carry out a promise oft repeated
To see that never would our stack of cord
wood be depleted?
At this late date to get from Keith
Such stuff as well-dried wood
Is asking more than he can do,
However much he should.
If dryad's fear or wood nymph's dear
Has stilled the Hopkins saw
Then bring another promised cord
That's cut. We'll say no more.
With grief we'll look elsewhere for oak;
Till found, we'll sit and freeze,
While Hopkinses before a blaze
Are snug in new-found ease.
If you had let us know before,
We'd asked Keith then for fuel.
To tell us now, as winter comes,
Approximates the cruel.
As snows fall fast and winter's blast
Makes even dryads shiver,
We'll woodless sit and slowly freeze
And blame it on Sam's liver.

* * *

We had a great intellectual ferment on Partington Ridge this last week. Nick had heard Olivier doing Hamlet on the radio and couldn't believe his ears when Sir Laurence got to the "Alas, poor Yorick" speech. So he looked it up in his Kittredge Shakespeare and subsequently in *five* other editions before he could be convinced that he, Nicholas Roosevelt, erstwhile pupil of the great Kittredge himself, had been misquoting the second line for all these years. So he quizzed Tirzah (his wife) who also flubbed the dub. Determined to find out if they were the only dummies on the ridge they went around quizzing everybody else, saying sternly, "What comes after 'Alas, poor Yorick?'" *Everyone* flubbed the dub, including such prideful scholars as David Tolerton and Henry Miller. Only lumpy, dumpy, dishwashy, harassed Nancy Hopkins was able to save the day and solve the riddle; I have been named the Brain Queen of the Ridge. Don't you think that is quite a distinction?

* * *

Charlie Levitzky and I are plunging into the Beethoven sonatas this winter, and it really is an education for me, for both he and Melissa are very knowledgeable about how Beethoven ought to be played. It is odd and wonderful that we have living here in Big Sur two pianists (both men and both about forty or maybe less) who are better pianists than I have ever played with in the Bay Area. So it bodes well for the musical education of our children, if they ever wish to study the piano.

* * *

The garden is very seedy. I am not as worthy as you in that respect; my green thumb drops off about October and from then until April or May the very thought of a green, growing thing almost turns my stomach. Winter for me is a time for books and contemplation and idle rambles in the woods and tea-by-the-fire at four; then by spring I have gathered my forces for a new assault upon the forces of nature. Back to the seed-beds and hedge-rows! Down with sow bugs! Up with lettuces! Down with sloth! Up with determination and exhaustion!

January 1954

The children enjoyed the Christmas holiday enormously…the festivities seemed to keep on for the entire week following the Day for of course there was much wining and dining and feting. We actually had a string quartet for one entire day down at a neighbor's house…of course I sandwiched the care of the children in between the music so at times the quartet perforce became a trio. But it was lots of fun.

Alfhild and Gustave Overstrom

Alfhild Overstrom had a patented homestead claim on 120 acres on the high ridge to the south of Partington Creek. Alfhild had applied for the claim as a single woman in 1927, the same year she married Gustave Overstrom, and the claim was patented in her married name in 1937.

Gustave was a skilled woodworker. Together with Sam Trotter and other early Big Sur residents, Gustave felled several redwoods from the canyon and hewed them into lumber sufficient to make a small cabin and barn. Simple and beautiful interior cabinetry, all hand-hewn and carefully smoothed, still functions today as testament to Gustave's skill.

* * *

The Overstroms, the old Swedish couple with the cabin on the ridge south of ours, came up from Los Angeles to spend the holidays. So all of us who love them dearly had to make the ten-mile-round-trip pilgrimage afoot up the old county trail to their hilltop. Sam, Clem, Emile and I went together, having left the girls with a babysitter for the day. Naturally I was no asset to have along, being so lumpy and dumpy; but Emile is slow, too, having a clubfoot. The Overstroms were as fine as ever and treated us to such a tremendous Swedish spread that we couldn't rise from the table for almost two hours. And even then Mrs. Overstrom surveyed the food that was left and frowned and vociferously deplored the fact that we "weren't hungry."

Gustave is 84 now, but looks 20 years younger…certainly he hasn't aged a day since I first met him five years ago. And Alfhild! She is only a comparative stripling in her late sixties or so, but what strength…what vigor! It pleases me to know that she is one of 12 brothers and sisters and every one of the brood is still alive and thriving. Aren't Swedes wonderful?

* * *

I am reading a marvelous book, Thomas Mann's *The Magic Mountain*, and as always when I get into a good work I simply cannot put it down. It is a massive work and one that in many ways I am intensely critical of and yet it is *good*. So I carry it around everywhere with me and snatch a few minutes with it whenever I can. I have formed the habit of always carrying a book with me when I go out with the youngsters…then when they get absorbed in some activity or game I swish the book out and read a chapter or so until their cries indicate a crisis…much more reading gets done that way.

Even in weather that is drippy like today we bundle up and spend a few hours out in the cold and mist, and the little girls return home with rosy cheeks and noses and none of us at all the worse for all the wetness.

* * *

Things have been popping here in Big Sur. Henry Miller up and married his Eve with whom he has been living for a year or two…people say "Why does Henry want to marry at all?" and we surmise that he wants a housekeeper and the housekeeper wants to be made an honest woman. I must say that she certainly works hard for him…does all the repair work and terrace-laying and housekeeping and cares for his two children who are spending this year with them. Eve, in fact, adores Val and Tony as though they were her own and is a wonderful mother to them…she will miss them dreadfully when their mother takes them south again next year, but perhaps by that time Eve will fill a cradle of her own, if Henry will let her.

February 1954

We have been reading a lot lately…mostly in the evenings. I go to bed fairly early these days, for Darien hits the deck well before the crack of dawn and insists on rousing Jory right away by hammering on her wall with both fists shouting, "Play now, Jory!"

The girls are sitting in front of the fire right now happily fortified by heaping bowls of popcorn which we have just made; the time is 4:30 and the rain seems to have temporarily stopped. Just an hour ago there was thunder and lightning. They both are dressed for a party; the idea is theirs, not mine. Goodness me, they are feminine to the core! Nothing will do but they must wear dresses *all* the time now; and since Jory is able to dress herself and her little sister I can't prevent the donning of finery. The minute my back is turned they are into the closet and out come organdy frocks and Mary Jane slippers, though it be snowing outside and freezing inside.

Away with ugly, sensible overalls and sweaters and thick stockings! On with frail nylon slips and frothy pinafores and slick silk socks!

* * *

Sam just came in with 42 eggs that were laid yesterday and today. Whatever are we going to do with them all? We sell some…obviously we are going to have to take on a few more customers.

March 1954

Summer months are a grand time to take other people's children for the day while their parents go to town or such and give my own the benefit of some older companionship, but keeping an eye on a gang of children is quite time-consuming. However, I love it…the more the merrier. Last Sunday I had a merry little crew indeed…a friend came up in the morning to help Sam lay pipe (he is a plumber by trade so is a very useful friend at times!) and brought his two boys aged six and nine to get them off his wife's hands for a while. Then at noontime Maud Oakes brought Tony and Val Miller and another child up for a picnic lunch and as she had to return home later to work in her garden I suggested she leave the kids all afternoon and let me take them back down the hill at suppertime. So believe me did things pop all afternoon! We had a wonderful time, though the six older ones managed to get in lots of mischief at times when Darien would take over my attention. Sam asked me later how so much damage happened to get done…gate latches broken, plants crushed, tools flung into the swimming pool. "Weren't you watching those kids?" he asked. I could only meekly state that it was almost impossible to keep my eyes on six healthy boys and girls who were surging from the swings to the alfalfa field to the chicken house and back again to the wine cellar and the lumber pile and the bars, what with having also to watch a two-year-old who wasn't up to racing with the gang.

* * *

Darien is really a handful at this point. She is trying to grow up so fast and do everything "by self" which ends up with everything in a terrible snarl. She has very firm ideas about what she will and will not wear. Should this be the night when only green pajamas are clean and available, then this must inevitably be the night when she Will Wear NOTHING BUT LELLOW JAMAS! Sam and I would be frantic if the whole thing didn't strike us as so funny. It starts when I call, "Bath now, Darien!" Immediately there is rage and a flood of angry protest and invective (she cannot abide water at this point). But screaming and kicking she is subjected to a sponge bath and the pajamas are brought forth…she scrutinizes them intently to ascertain the color, then immediately demands another color, which inevitably is unavailable. Oh, the raging then, the utter fury, the wails, the kicks, while Sam and I marvel at the intensity of this ever-repeated scene. Of course it is just a stage which will pass like the others; and certainly once I have squeezed

The Grange Hall

The Big Sur Grange Hall was built in 1950. The building, centrally located in the Big Sur Valley, served as a simple but vibrant community center for potlucks, meetings, dances, movies, school festivities and theatrical performances. The main auditorium has a raised stage at one end (complete with "dressing rooms" in the wings) and ample floor space that in the 1950s could be filled with folding chairs to hold rapt audiences for movie night or livened with decorations and a local Santa to delight children at Christmas or cleared out to accommodate swirling couples in a square dance. Adjacent to the auditorium is a smaller room where food can be served—usually potluck style—for any of the Grange Hall's various community gatherings. Today, the Grange Hall continues to function as a community center hosting films, potlucks, community meetings, occasional theatrical events and seasonal craft shows.

The Big Sur Grange, which was chartered in 1948, put on the "Potluck Revues" in the 1950s to raise funds. Immense community effort and artistic creativity went into these productions. In 1955, the Grange also started a monthly community newsletter, the *Big Sur Round-up*, that has been faithfully published ever since, sharing local news, announcements, homegrown poetry and community debate.

Walter Trotter hams it up at the Revue

and poured her into the wrong pajamas she is suddenly once more the rosy, appealing little angel she always has been…she just needs that one moment of self-assertion. But you can imagine how it drains the energies of fat, eight-months-pregnant Mommy!

* * *

Last night was the Big Sur Revue, and it was really wonderful. Of course we think the annual variety show is the funniest thing ever…but perhaps knowing everyone involved makes it seem funnier to us. About half of Big Sur is on the stage, and somehow enough people are left over to completely pack the hall on both nights…of course quite a few people come down from town for it, for it is becoming quite a famous event in the county.

We had descended the mountain in a terrific hail-and-thunder-and-lightning storm, but we wouldn't have missed it for the world. I was left with the impression that Big Sur has more than its share of big people…there was a terribly funny number of a women's modern dance class (rather à la Martha Graham) made up of all the really fat women in the countryside. Sam nearly died laughing. And by the time they got some of our local *men* on the stage…Walter Trotter and Billy Post and Franklin Peace and a few others…all of them well-built but nothing less than Herculean…it was really something. In the final act they were all dressed up in little nightcaps and long white nightgowns, each hugging some ragged, worn Teddy bear or doll to his bosom, and carrying candles in a little bedtime march that was completely captivating…somehow those tremendous men managed to catch for a moment the very gestures and charm of childhood.

Four

"The more I live in this so lovely mountain area the more I appreciate the people who also have chosen to live here."

In 1954, when I, the third child, was born there still was no residential phone service in Big Sur. People communicated face-to-face — stopping by friends' homes on the way to or from town, meeting the mailman (and other neighbors) for the daily mail delivery at the mail boxes along the highway, or dropping in at Post's Rancho Sierra Mar restaurant, the café that served as the community gathering place for many years. This regular personal contact fostered a deep sense of community and interdependence, something that was lost once the phones reached every home.

A lively figure helping unite the community was Ed the mailman. For some 20 years, Ed Culver took his postal mission to the limit. Along with the daily mail, Ed delivered groceries, prescriptions and laundry, offered rides to those who needed them, and brought the latest news on the local weather. When slides closed the highway he made sure that liquor got through to those who needed it. And he talked. Six days a week, anyone who felt a little lonely at Partington could go down to the highway to wait along with other ridge neighbors for Ed and his cheerful banter.

May 1954

I don't understand it, but it is true that the more babies you have the more each one delights you. How do women ever stop having them? I just can't believe at this point that I would ever be able to say, "This one is to be the last one." Really, Heidi is a dear character and it seems strange to think that she has not always been with us…certainly we cannot now imagine life without her.

I had Heidi lying on our bed the other day and went out of the house for something. When I returned Jory was curled up there beside her and I overheard her confiding to Heidi "…and I'll teach you to play on the bars and hang by your knees and play in the sand pile and swim and *everything*…"

* * *

Spring has been delicious. Each season has such delights here; we never can decide which one holds the greatest riches. Winter is cozy and exciting and snug by the fire, with violent storms, horrendous south winds, rain pelting down for days at a time, and then serenely green hills and long clear days and the ocean glassy for fishing; we love every bit of it. But after all those months of indoor evenings and fires it seems wonderful to be able to move out onto the porch

Hunting

Nan writes enthusiastically about hunting in 1954, but it came hard at first. One story that was *not* included in her letters was that just weeks after they were married, Sam strode proudly down the mountain with a buck slung over his back, and Nan's reaction was to burst into tears—the first in their relationship. It didn't take long, however, for her to come around.

We all loved the meat, which might be tough but was so richly flavorful. Nothing better than a salty, crisp-skinned pigeon on the plate or dark-gravied venison stew! "Roast wild duck is my favorite food in all the world," wrote Nan. "Sam says that watching me plunge greedily into one is a treat in itself." It was always understood that the best meat—the duck, the abalone, the heart of the deer—was reserved for Nan.

A keenly observant lay naturalist, Sam was a natural hunter. He found something akin to spiritual joy in successfully tracking "the wily buck" through the steep draws and stickery thickets of the Coast Ridge. He hunted alone or in close cooperation with a trusted friend. After an evening of oiling his gun and manufacturing his own bullets, Sam left early and hiked hard into the heat of the day. Whether he was successful or not, he always was happy when he returned from the hunt—hot, dusty, disheveled and smelling wonderfully of the pungent turpentine weed that blooms in late August in the high dry meadows.

for meals and enjoy the freshness of the out-of-doors and the hum of insects and the bird songs that make us want to linger for hours over our breakfast coffee.

* * *

We lost a chicken to a bobcat the other afternoon…we heard all the fracas and found a trail of feathers going down into the canyon, so Sam pursued the villain while I ran for his gun, but still the cat got away and we didn't even recover the hen. Now I am afraid that the cat will remember his happy hunting ground and return.

June 1954

A friend stopped by on his way to Santa Barbara. He had intended to "phone" to see if we were home and of course was astonished to find that some areas in California still manage to survive without that ubiquitous instrument of the modern age. But he drove up and found me and the girls home. Being a financial manager, he is interested in helping us be more Sensible of the Future, and I had a momentary thought that he must be Daddy's idea of the Wise Young Man while Sam must seem like the Foolish Grasshopper who sang all summer and had no Grain stored against the Winter. But believe me, I wouldn't trade! Nor would I exchange one pinch of our foolishness for one mountain of his wisdom. The more I live in this so lovely mountain area the more I appreciate the people who also have chosen to live here…all of them are so very different from each other and yet so splendidly interesting and vibrant in his own way.

Country living is so clean and good and instinctive. The more I see of our city friends the more I appreciate the radiant, random sort of health that our friends here in the country enjoy…you feel an ebullience about them and a splendid sort of vitality, men and women both, which I suppose must come from the outdoor life and perhaps just the slower pace of living.

August 1954

Now visits are through for the year…we try to see the people that we want to see in June and July, for this coming weekend the deer season starts and goes on until the middle of September, and we keep our beds free for such friends as Pete and Keith who can only hunt on weekends. I enjoy this "man's" time of year very much; I enjoy cooking for them and hearing their plans for and later accounts of the hunts and helping them package the venison. It is a unique time of year here in the country and to me has come rather to mark the end of the summer season and the beginning of fall.

I must stop now and get my rolls into the oven to bake…they have risen to a fabulous mountain. This week I will fill the freezer against hunting season so that I will be able to bring forth man-size meals on the spur of the moment…I can never be sure how many hungry hunters I shall suddenly be called upon to feed, and I have learned from experience that nothing so pleases them as hot breads and PIES.

* * *

All is well here. Heidi is blooming and getting huge and very active. Right now she is playing on the porch with Jory and Darien and I see that Darien is trying to feed her a raisin. She will certainly grow up like Topsy and I'm sure be all the better for it; if we're not forever fussing at them they seem to survive and be much better natured than otherwise.

September 1954

The girls have lately developed a new game that I dread. It is called "taking a trip" and consists of dragging into their room every available box and carton and filling them with all their belongings, of course helter-skelter. So bureaus are emptied, book shelves are laid bare, the toy chest is ransacked, the closet is denuded…and all is heaved into the boxes to form one great stew. This done, the fun is over…who picks up? Poor Old Mommy. Naturally I insist that they help put away, but such a gigantic task (and, believe me, it *is* a gigantic task!) is beyond the concentrating powers of a two-year-old and even reduces a four-year-old to tears of exhaustion…of course P.O.M. is supposed to be Superwoman! But such is life.

October 1954

There was a bad fire about twenty miles north of us this last week…it burned from Boucher's Gap down to the Little Sur River, where they finally got it out just before it reached the new Boy Scout Camp…a prevailing north breeze kept it from moving onto Chapman's ranch (where Frank Trotter is foreman), but Frank was very busy putting roads in with his bulldozer which could be used for backfiring or even for escape for the families if necessary. The fire burned for six days, and of course everyone was anxious for firsthand news of it, for each ranch threatened or partly burned over seems to be in some way personally connected with all the rest of us. Clem and Emile reported when they came up here Wednesday evening they had driven up to Frank's to see what the situation was, and encountered no less than thirty-one people (including thirteen children) in the Trotters' tiny living-room, all of them having arrived on just the same errand. Fern was in her element, for if there is anything in this world that Fern loves it is lots of people!

Really, Fern is one of the gems of this world, and volumes could be written about her. It is always a joy to call on the Trotters just because we know (and everyone else knows, too) that Fern will be waiting on the porch eagerly, having heard the car approaching from far down the

Dinner with Frank and Fern

canyon, and will rush out, all wispy and grease-bespattered from her kitchen chores, with great hugs for everyone and the joyfully shouted information that we are the Very People she had been Longing to see…and there is no hypocrisy in it, no matter who arrives, for Fern Longs to see Everyone. And it makes no difference if a great crowd arrives just as the family is sitting down to dinner, for Fern always prepares enough for an army. But then she is always cooking for seven anyway, and there are invariably several other children there spending the night (or the month) so a few more makes no difference at all.

The fire made us think seriously about what steps to take in case of fire here…it is unlikely that it would be burning down from the ridge, for it goes very slowly downhill, and most likely that it would come up from the Partington Canyon side, where there are so many houses and more people along the road. But that would be the worst side for us, for of course it would be impossible to escape down the road. So we have talked out the routine we would follow…sprinklers on, butane turned off, girls under wet blankets in the middle of the alfalfa field, which is the widest clearing…if time, then guns and fiddles with girls. Fortunately, our only valuables are portable. We do have a fire hose which would be good for wetting down the house and surrounding trees, but I am not strong enough to wield it under pressure so if Sam weren't home it would be next to useless. Anyway, we hope we never have to face a fire.

[Note: Turning on all the sprinklers and wetting down the property in advance of a fire is generally considered futile. The water should be saved to put out the fire once the fire's front has passed over. We know better now!]

* * *

Sam is off fire-fighting tonight. The fire is still burning some twenty miles north of us or so; they had it out by Friday, but it started up again that night and today a hot dry wind came up and things are really bad. We heard the local news at noon over the radio, and it said that 700 men are already on the fire-line and the fire was breaking away to the north. Sam had been over-hauling the tractor today, and when he went back out after lunch I had a hunch that he would want to go…that is part of his nature…the desire to do battle when battle is in a noble cause, to come to grips with the essence of manhood by pitting personal skill and strength against danger; it is so Sam to the core that I cannot think of him apart from that quality. He worked like a mad thing at the tractor until about three, and then couldn't resist that plume of smoke on the horizon any longer…off he went, and we will miss him until he returns. It is the same impulse that makes him want to tackle our treacherous south coast surf in the kayak…the fish he brings home are just a by-product of the challenge and the excitement. His mother is always working on me to make him give up such things as kayaking and mountain-climbing and tree-felling and, in fact, everything he does here in the country. "If you ask him not to, you know he will never do those things again, Nancy." But I can only answer that it is his nature to do those things. If he didn't, he might be just as fine but he wouldn't for a minute be Sam. And some-how I feel strongly that one shouldn't tamper with other people's natures.

* * *

Summer *is* a lovely time, and we have enjoyed this last one more than I can say. Now we feel the restlessness in the air and know that the first winter storm cannot be more than a couple of weeks away. But this is still Indian summer, with our grapes all ripe and sweet and sun-warmed on the vines and the children forever foraging in the fig tree and clambering down all stained and sticky from head to toe. And it makes us sad to think that the evenings will soon be cold, so we clutch every moment as we can…tuck Heidi into bed just before sunset and then we four oldsters go swimming as darkness falls, plunging and shouting in the water, feeling a million miles away from everything in the shadowed water, and running shivering up to the house, cleansed and exultant and very, very hungry, for a late supper of venison or trout or pigeon.

* * *

[Sam's rainfall record]

> *Beautiful summer—no excessive heat. Almost continual low baromenter (Pacific*
> *high—whereabouts unknown). As of today (Oct. 24) fall also mild, pleasant.*
> *Ocean rough. No "dog days." Boating poor. Good crop of madrone berries. Pigeons*
> *on ridge. Deer season favorable. 7 bucks, first used scope. Still swimming in pool.*
> *Land dry, springs low.*

* * *

The fire that I last wrote to you about is finally out. It was a terribly destructive thing, though only one home was lost. It certainly will cause a lot of erosion in that area and ruin the watershed for a few years to come. Last weekend when Sam went to volunteer he ended up at Chapman's ranch where he had a ringside seat. The entire opposite ridge was a mass of flame as far as the eye could see. Before the evening he and Frank had driven down over the newly bulldozed road past Boucher's Gap (where the fire started) to the Little Sur River where they were making a last-ditch stand to save the Boy Scout Camp. They were backfiring right at the river and Sam said that the flames shot up those giant redwoods as up matchsticks. Of course the wildlife suffered terribly…they get so panicky and bolt right back into the flames. Then, too, the deer's coats catch fire and they rush out into the surrounding countryside and start fires in hundreds of new places. A fire is certainly a terrible thing.

* * *

Nick and Tirzah Roosevelt came up yesterday for a visit…Nick has come into possession of a 'cello and he is practicing madly and as excited as a child with great vistas opening up. He had brought the 'cello with him, and played on it for me. My, he plays well! His tone is round and resonant and wonderful, and he is honestly the only person I have ever played with who plays, to my mind, Perfectly in Tune (a thing I *never* do!). He left some music with me, and on Saturday afternoon we have a date with some duets. Heidi goes down for a nap about 3:30 or 4 so I shall immediately fly down to his house (three miles in the country seems practically "next door") and let Jory and Darien tag after Sam around home.

* * *

Sam worked this week on the starting of the Nolan house…these house-buildings are really men's social affairs, though all of them have to work like beavers. Sam came back with great stories of Frank Trotter's fabulous endurance…he is such a giant that he effortlessly exhausted all of the other men. Where they would stagger under one sack of cement, Frank would trot about with one under each arm as though he were merely dandling two cozy babies. But he is so completely unaware that his strength is anything out of the ordinary. You've never seen anything like the Trotter boys for sheer bulk and working capacity.

* * *

Friday was the school Halloween party, and all the small fry of the countryside attended in costume, with all sorts of traditional games and enough to eat to kill off all of them (so far no fatalities reported, however!). This community is so small that all the children long for *every* child to be there, whether or not he is of school age.

Pianist Gene Perrine, who attended the Boston Conservatory of Music, joined Nick and Nan to play trios at Nick's home. Gene and his partner, Bob Skiles, taught music and art (respectively) at Pfeiffer School and helped produce the Big Sur Revue. Later in the 1960s, Gene and Bob created and produced the summertime "Little Lyric Theater" involving coast children in imaginative, colorful, musical productions.

Today the girls attended a birthday party at Post's ranch...what food was consumed and wild games went on! After the games the children swarmed up on the hill by the barn to watch the skinning of the pigs...and I think it was the highlight of the party for them. It really is quite a difficult procedure, for the animals have to be scalded and shaved and such. But what lovely hams and bacons the Posts will get from them! They really use everything...even the heads and tripe.

* * *

Yesterday afternoon I played duets with Nick for an hour (Sam was home with the kids...Heidi napping) and we are certainly a good team. It was such fun. We shall play again next weekend, for Nick is so very enthusiastic about it...and Charlie Levitsky will play with us...string trio.

How odd it is that we live so far in the country and yet there are two musical groups that clamor for my genius (!?) and each wants to play once a week, which is all I could possibly do in town. And what makes it even more interesting is how different we all are and yet how much we like each other: Emile a farm boy with the greatest thing in his life being simply nature, and Clem from some vague Chicago background of Catholicism and then rebellion from it all when he was just on the brink of priesthood, and Nick who was "to the manor born" and educated in the finest tradition of Western civilization, and Charlie who is the urban Jewish intellectual from a Brooklyn immigrant family, magnificently self-educated, and his wife who is very American and excitable and reads tremendously (I honestly think that she and Charlie read more than anyone I know). And then me, of course. Aren't we weird and fabulous? Big Sur doesn't know what to make of this longhair swing.

November 1954

We seem to be in the throes of our first storm of the year…a strong south wind blowing and rain starting. Sam rushed down to Harry Dick's house early in the morning to return him a motor we had borrowed, for he feared that Harry Dick might need it and we couldn't return it once the rain really started. He found the lower ridge in great turmoil with everybody else rushing around returning things and getting things undercover and everyone of course stopping in at the Rosses for a cup of coffee and a discussion of barometric pressures…somehow the coming of winter is always a very exciting thing on the coast and always seems to take us unawares in spite of the fact that we know its coming is inevitable and irrevocable.

* * *

This weekend a hunting friend of Sam's stayed with us, and yesterday he and Sam poured a concrete slab for a barn-storeroom we are putting out by the point…it will be used to store grain and tools and such, and we will add to it to make a shelter for animals. The men had their shotguns beside them as they worked and every time a flight of pigeons came over they leaped for their weapons. They certainly are a good work team; they go like mad things. After a few glasses of wine for lunch they felt so peppy that they zipped up the canyon, felled a huge tan oak, and had a cord of wood split and stacked in no time at all. Of course Jory and Darien sneaked down to the point in the afternoon and pranced naughtily around the newly-poured slab, so now their little footprints are immortalized in the concrete…barefooted at that!

* * *

We get a treat this weekend; Clem and Emile have invited us to go with them to hear Szigeti play a sonata concert in Carmel. My one-of-several-favorite-men Cal is going to baby-sit for us. He is one of the coast's most capable baby-sitters; many is the time he has taken over the whole

Cal Calloway

Everyone in Big Sur knew Cal Calloway, whose heart was as big and tall as his lanky, six-foot frame. An electrician by training, he wired many of the early coast homes and often accepted no payment for the service. He loved children and took numbers of Big Sur kids to enjoy the Salinas rodeo. He worked for a time as the U.S. Forest Service backcountry ranger in the Los Padres National Forest and also worked as devoted ranch hand at Jo Chapman's Rancho Calera.

Trotter brood (all eight of the cousins) while Frank and Walter and their wives step out. He can warm a mean bottle and change didies as well as any woman…which is wonderful when you consider what a big, strapping, man's man he is. The girls love him dearly, as do Sam and I. We couldn't have a finer neighbor, and the more we see of him the more impressed we are with his essential loftiness. There isn't a fragment of pettiness in the man. He treats every human being from the oldest down to the tiniest baby as though they merited infinite respect and infinite courtesy. He never holds the slightest grudge against anyone; he is completely tolerant of all ways of life, but there is nothing wishy-washy about him when it comes to adhering to his own standards. Cal is the only one I can think of who really measures up to a heroic stature.

* * *

Our Partington trio is now a firmly established thing, with both Charlie and Nick fairly bouncing with enthusiasm. We meet at the Roosevelts' on Friday afternoons for an hour (while Heidi naps, bless her sweet self!). I don't know *when* I have seen Nick so happy…he is radiant, and it seems a shame that he didn't renew his interest in chamber music before this. We both love to twit Charlie, who gets very overly-confident when he has a glass of wine in him and then is apt to quail before the fifth position; Nick rallies him with endless Shakespeare quotations (he studied the Bard under Kittredge at Harvard) such as, "Rouse thy vaunting veins, boy; bristle thy courage up."

* * *

We had to chuckle at your account of Election Boards and such…we have a marvelous Election Board here in Big Sur. We vote at the Grange Hall, and of course it is Old Home Week since everyone knows everyone else. The officials (all women) sit and knit all day exactly like so many Madame de Farges. For some reason they have a list posted of everyone's political affiliation, and everyone is always amused to see how some of the families are split…Fern is a Democrat and Frank a Republican, for instance. Perl Smith and his wife are the only Socialists in Big Sur, and we all cherish their presence…they are real "old coast" people.

* * *

We took a hike up to Overstroms' with Clem and Emile. It was one of those lovely crisp blue November days, very still and delicious. It is a three-hour trip there, so we arrived at lunchtime, and it just happened to be Mrs. Overstrom's baking day. So there was hot, heavenly Swedish bread for lunch, and we all ate phenomenally and drank copiously of the gallon of wine Sam had toted up, and Mr. Overstrom told story after marvelous story of Swedes and their absurdities…after lunch the stories went on while we lounged under their old apple trees and watched Sam and Clem move a few square yards of the rocky hillside with pick and wheelbarrow…then when the sun was getting dangerously low in the sky we realized that we had to get back before dark (Mr. Overstrom of course insisted that it was "much too late" to even think of returning until the next day) and fairly flew back down the trail. Sam dashed on ahead straight down the hill instead of following the trail, and it was well that he did because of course us foolish four loiterers were caught in complete darkness before we had even worked our way to the north fork…the bridge across the middle fork is a six-inch log that spans the rushing stream about ten feet above the water…we had tight-roped it in the morning, but in the darkness had to sit down and inch our way across it…it was so dark we couldn't even see the water, but we could hear it! Sam met us at the north fork with flashlights which he had brought from the jeep, and we finished the trip very tired and very gay and happy.

* * *

Last night we had dinner with the Tolertons…it was a delightful evening. David's wife is a superb cook…with no effort at all she makes leftovers into the most artistic of dinners, and their house is arranged so that the dining table is right beside a little fireplace which is very pleasant, especially on a cold night. In the evening David regaled us with peeks into the past…he has all sorts of old Caruso and MacCormack and Chaliapin records which have such an inimitable flavor of the early decades of this century. David was born in 1907, so was a child during the heyday of those artists; his parents were great theatre-goers and always took David from the time he was five years old. So he has a wonderful child's-eye-view of Caruso and MacCormack and Sarah Bernhardt and Nijinsky and the rest of that era. It is fascinating to hear him tell of those things, for he is a great raconteur.

David talks so brilliantly on so many and varied subjects that Sam and I, knowing nothing of what he was talking about, couldn't have presumed to keep up any kind of conversation. I wish we could have had his conversation recorded somehow…poets, painters, architects, philosophers, educationists, ideas, ideas, ideas spilled so kaleidoscopically from him that we were completely dazed and dazzled. And David (oh, how I love him!) makes his brilliant statements with such an air of authority that one can never dispute his decisions.

December 1954

[letter from Sam]

Today was the opening of pigeon season so I roused myself at 5 and, fortified with peanuts, made my way to Cold Spring. The climb up the hill was made in complete darkness. If I had not been so familiar with the trail I am sure I would have ended in some dank gully. Having often hiked at night without a flashlight I started off blithely only to discover that it is easy enough to travel by moonlight or even by starlight but making one's way under heavy clouds on a moonless night is a different matter. My most compelling thought was of the yuccas, several of which grow by the trail. However, I arrived at the divide we call Massacre Ridge without too much trouble. The pigeons, on the other hand, did not arrive. So the few of us who were there stood around and shivered for several hours and then went home.

* * *

Somehow from December to June we are such rabid picnickers…you'd think that living in the country we would get our fill of rural spots, and yet at least once a week we have a major outing (meaning an all-day affair) either at a beach or back in the mountains somewhere. Yesterday we took an excursion up to Boucher's Gap (the divide that separates Rocky Creek from the Little Sur watershed) and ate our lunch on the most heavenly little flat imaginable,

Sam with Little Sur River steelhead

with miles and miles of the Little Sur backcountry lying far below us and Mt. Pico Blanco looming on our right. The Rosses were with us, and it seems to me that we ate for hours…hard rolls and salami and pickles and potato salad and cold lamb and fresh home-made bread and green onions and wine and coffee and cold beer. All in all, it was a most lovely day…we returned home at sunset sunburned and very full and happy.

If this good weather holds out and the rushing waters of the Little Sur subside, Sam and Harry Dick are going back there later this week with spears (and pistols) for the steelhead are running up the river. When the water is high and roiled it is too hard to spear them. They freeze well, and are wonderful eating. They run 2-3 feet long, so you can see that just one of them means a lot of meat!

* * *

We had a beautiful day for Darien's birthday, warm and clear and still…she does have such luck, considering her birthday comes at what should be such a stormy, cold time of year…for three birthdays now we have had glorious picnics to celebrate the event. This time we went for the day to the beach at the mouth of the Big Sur river, and the kids were in seventh heaven…they raced naked through the surf and paddled in the river and we all collected shells…that beach is very rich in them. Of course we had cake and ice cream and a wonderful al fresco lunch….

January 1955

It is raining this afternoon, so I am uncertain whether I shall brave the elements to go down to Nick's for piano quartets…but I know the others will be crushed if the viola does not appear, even though they can always play piano trios without me. I will try, I think, and just wear warm clothes and rubber boots so if I get stuck coming back up the hill I can walk up the hill to my friend Cal's house and get some aid.

We are working on the Beethoven and Schumann piano quartets…Charlie finds Schumann a bit beyond him but he tries bravely. Gene Perrine, our pianist, is superb…*never* have I played with such a pianist. I can tell just from the sensitive way he plays exactly which beat of the measure he is on. Nick plays marvelously, and has that pleasant 'cellist's characteristic of simply playing what is set before him and never quibbling about the difficulty of the piece or the impossibility of the tempo…he is affability itself, which is rather different from the violinist's temperament demonstrated by Charlie…Charlie is always enthusing on the heights or else groveling in the depths…he never strikes a happy medium. But I love him dearly…I wouldn't have these violinists any different!

* * *

The girls are fine…Jory and Darien are going through the most delicious stage of politeness…it is all "may I be excused?" and "thank you for the lovely time," which just about bowls over some of our more crusty friends. One evening we stopped in to call at Cal's house on the way home and as we left him Darien called out so sweetly, "Goodbye, goodbye; thank you for the lovely time." I thought Cal would drop dead from astonishment that his simple hospitality (a piece of candy for each girl) could call forth such histrionics!

February 1955

Tonight I am going to devote to the making of a colossal Valentine for our dear Cal…cutting out pictures from an old Monkey Ward catalogue and pasting them on with such sentiments as "you will think that I am 'nuts' but like a 'bolt' out of the blue my heart felt a 'wrench' when

I 'saw' you" etc. etc. I can go on in that vein almost forever, and Cal certainly rates a Valentine. Sam has promised to deliver it for me tomorrow rain or shine!

* * *

I don't quite know how to break the news to you gently that yet another babe will arrive in August…I can just see the wrath and consternation sitting upon your parental brows. Will you forgive us? We are both excited and delighted…it seems as though the more you have the more you want. But I can just hear Daddy saying sternly, "Enough is enough."

How all the local men roared when it was announced that Nancy Hopkins would produce in August! "Well, Hopkins, not much hunting *this* year!" It just isn't done for Big Sur wives to have babies in August; I have often laughed to Sam that he must have been really smitten to have agreed to an August wedding…of course at that time I understood not at all the significance of the month of August!

* * *

Sam wants me to tell you that we harvested a cauliflower in our garden this week that weighed seven-and-a-half pounds and measured roughly a foot-and-a-half in diameter. Isn't that colossal?

* * *

We had a big coast wedding this past Saturday. Everyone for miles around was there to wish Billy Post well. Friday had been dark and cold, but Saturday dawned gloriously with a great dramatic sea of fog suddenly dispersing and leaving the coastal mountains bright and fresh and deliciously green and warm. The five of us sallied forth in great finery for the occasion, the girls looking like three little angels (Heidi in dotted Swiss quite like a strawberry ice cream cone) and Sam all wedged into a starched collar and necktie. But when we saw the finery at the Grange Hall, we were abashed…such tiny, flower-bedecked hats; such crisp, chic veils; such pastel suits and frothy dickies; such carnation-whitened buttonholes; such organdy pinafores and pomaded hair; Big Sur has never put quite *such* a face forward. The Grange Hall had miraculously become church-like, with an altar and flowers and an organ. The place was packed, with even the standing room crowded. And Lynn was the pièce de résistance in a really beautiful white satin gown that I understand she made herself.

It was a tremendous event, perfect in every detail, and I don't know when the coast has had such a thoroughly rip-roaring time…such a shame that Billy only gets married once! The drinking and wassailing went on all through the next day and night, though we left after only three hours or so of it. It was a cataclysmic occasion…from the bonnets and pomade right down to the time we left when Butch Netland passed out, his Stetson still on his head. No, it seems there is nothing quite like a country wedding.

* * *

Yesterday Cal put on a huge spread…we ate all afternoon…his "lady-friend" was down from Monterey and his daughter and her family were up from San Luis Obispo, and at the last moment the Rosses happened to drive by with some friends of theirs, on the way up to see us…so we hailed them all in and they ate too…somehow in the country there always seems to be plenty for everyone. It was very gay, and the girls loved that afternoon too because Cal saddled up the horses and took them for a long ride.

* * *

This is a lovely rainy weekend, with all of us indoors busy about various things. Sam spent the morning down on the lower road with Cal filling in holes with gravel; they intended to work again this afternoon but the rain is harder and they called it off. The girls have been madly dressing up and impersonating a series of the most fantastic characters; a little while ago Darien was dressed up as a "clown" (*her* version of a clown, which is quite unique) and Jory was swathed in scarves and had feathers in her hair…she was an Indian. The game consisted of Darien chasing Jory around the room belaboring her with a Teddy bear and shouting, "Go back to the woods! Go back to the woods!" Though their games seem quite primitive, they put great verve into them. Lately Darien has taken to impersonating a character that she labels "the merry virgin"

Dressing up

which I can only surmise she has derived from Christmas and the Holy Family. It convulses Sam, of course, and he is very careful that she doesn't get the nomenclature straightened out.

Darien's personality is emerging more and more clearly as time goes on, and we can only catalogue her affectionately as a "complete screwball." She goes from thing to thing quite like a drunken thing, as the caprice seizes her. She will be roaring with laughter, weeping disconsolately, stamping her little foot in rage, and smothering us with hugs and kisses, all within the short space of two minutes. It exhausts us just to keep up with her emotional changes. She goes through her meals in quite the same way; can't wait to get to the table, professing to be ravaged by hunger, bolts down one pea, begs for "zert," assures us she is stuffed and "maybe I scused" and off she goes to another round of insane play. All this happens before the rest of us have even *started* on our meal; it gives us indigestion to watch her…we really can't enjoy our food until she is safely down from the table.

We don't try to change her, because she seems to us so peculiarly lovable just as she is. With three children and a fourth coming, we feel rather amusedly that it will be fun to have a screwball in the crowd.

March 1955

We too saw the *Sunset* edition that featured that children's room…we have been subscribing to the magazine but have dropped our subscription so won't be getting it much longer. It made us feel conscience-stricken that we ought to be spending our time planning our Home more Efficiently instead of spending it in the many more foolish ways that we temperamentally find so indispensable. *Sunset* wants you to think of nothing else but Good Planning, whether it be in the realm of gardening or house-building or (most insidious of all) house-improving, which after all is something that *Sunset* considers must go on and on and on. So, as I say, Sam and I have surrendered. We lay down our arms, leave the field quite disgraced but unashamed, and repair to the beach and the flower-strewn backcountry, leaving our house an unthought-out shambles…we'll never make the cover of *Sunset*, but then neither will we develop ulcers trying to decide the very best ground-cover for a steep north exposure.

* * *

Jory and Darien are getting very tanned these days, scurrying around out of doors. Sam made them quite a creditable teeter-totter and they have a hysterically merry time on it. No accidents so far, though I have held my breath watching Darien fly up into the air like a rocket and barely manage to keep her balance in the process. As yet there are no handles on it; when

Sam gets those made I think there will be less danger of spills. They go swimming, too; Sam and I are not yet so brave.

* * *

Sam has reached the conclusion that I simply like complicated prose, and hence choose Henry James and Marcel Proust, the most difficult of all prose writers; that must be it. After all, in these years of raising small children, I often ponder the fact that the business of day-to-day living with a young brood taxes the nervous system, the emotional set-up, the intuition, the physical powers of endurance…everything, in short, but the mind, gets a daily work-out to keep it in good working order. But the poor mind! By the time we fondly wave farewell to our youngest chicken-child off to college and the world, our minds, if we have been conscientious mothers, have become completely vestigial organs! So perhaps when I crave this tussle with difficult prose it is simply some inner instinct warning me to keep that poor little member in some sort of working order so I can put it to use again some day. I don't quite manage to read daily, but as a friend of mine is so fond of saying about everything she doesn't get around to, "I *dream*."

[Sam's rainfall record]

Mar. 30	.25"	*A dry warm March. Hills turning brown!*
Apr. 17	.75"	*Almost too late to do any good.*
Apr. 18	.25"	
Apr. 20–21	2.35"	*Strongest wind of the year. This always happens when I scrape the road. Will the rain help the open slopes which are almost brown?*

April 1955

We too are enjoying the spring. The oaks sprout new growth amid the old, and the varied tints of dark and light green make the entire forest shimmer with an Impressionist light. The maples and sycamores and black oaks are coming out in leaf now, too, and the barren spots in the woods are becoming bright again. The madrones are white with blossoms now, and the wild lilac has been especially beautiful this year…away across the canyon we can pick out the spots of bright blue where they are blooming. Now the yuccas are pushing their huge red shoots upward and in another two weeks we ought to have their bright candles lighting the ridge above us…they rise sometimes to twelve feet in height, and their cream-colored blossoms have the most divine fragrance imaginable.

Spring flowers on the Coast Ridge

There was rain for the last two days, the first real rain in almost two months, so today Sam is scraping and grading our upper road, which is a job that must be done immediately after the last rain of the year while the ground is still somewhat moist. Our last mile of road is not oiled, so needs regular attention to keep it navigable during the wet months; the two miles below that is oiled, but is very bumpy and rutted nevertheless; a neighbor helps Sam maintain *that* stretch. It is quite a winter chore for him, but we feel that the isolation is well worth it…old unsociable us! But all the chores that keep him busy on our own acres mean that he is home a good deal, and we certainly enjoy the family life that gives us. And when he is back in the canyon felling trees and splitting wood or trail-building the girls love to walk to wherever he is working and watch him; they have gotten very independent about getting around the country by themselves, and they are cautious and quite sensible so I never worry about them.

* * *

Heidi was thrilled beyond measure at Sam's return from the hills…she loves her daddy. I was so touched when I went out to get wood from the porch beside her room early Sunday morning to build a fire with. She heard me stirring around out there and cried joyfully, "Dada! Dada!"

Post's Rancho Sierra Mar Restaurant

The Rancho Sierra Mar restaurant was built in 1945 and run by Irene Post and her daughter Mary. Referred to as "Post's" by all the locals, the restaurant for years served as the hub of the Big Sur community with Mary Post its most warm and welcoming hostess. "When you walked into Mary's place, you got elected to every office. Everything was done at Rancho Sierra Mar," said local resident Bette Somerville in an interview, recalling those early days.

Post's offered all the best in basic American food, notably the juicy hamburgers with their accompanying shaved "carrot curls" (Post's knew how to entice kids to eat veggies!) and sweet strawberry pies for dessert. It also provided space for regular card

games—as many as 40 people might gather to play hearts or poker—and offered leisurely counter space for coffee and conversation. It was the first place in Big Sur to boast a functioning TV. Even with reception so "snowy" you could hardly see the picture, Post's TV was immensely popular during baseball season.

She knows that he always comes out there first thing in the morning to get wood for the daily fire. Tonight she was up until 8 o'clock having the best time playing games with her sisters…oh, that every baby in this world could be the third!

* * *

Clem and Emile and we had a glorious hike across the Dani ranch down to the beach to Cooper Point, then along the beach for some miles, though we had to climb up over the headlands in several points for the tide was high. We had lunch at the mouth of the Big Sur river…wine and smoked whitefish and great hunks of jack cheese…then we climbed the hills of the Molera ranch back to their home on the ridge, gathering mushrooms as we went. It is such beautiful walking country on that block of land between the valley of the Big Sur and the sea. We got home to watch the brilliant colors and drink a welcome hot cup of coffee…the day had been nippy and marvelously clear, just after a storm. Then we picked up the girls and all seven of us went out to dinner at Post's which is the very coziest spot on the coast to eat out. It was such fun.

May 1955

We have had such rain for the last two weeks…off and on, of course, with hot summery days in between…but still quite some downpours. The garden I suspect is ge-finished…I cannot bear to inspect it closely. It never fails; each year I realize that it is utter folly to plant before May 15, and then each year I am completely deluded again by the hot weather we have in February and March.

* * *

It is a foggy day today after a week of scorching weather…a lovely change, but the girls are disappointed that they cannot go swimming. When it's hot, we swim every night at twilight after Heidi has been tucked in, and the girls love plunging around in the water in the gathering darkness…on evenings when it seems too cool to go to bed with wet hair we go for long walks in the hills instead. What a little brood of romantics we are going to hatch!

* * *

Yesterday was music day at Nick's, but since Sam wasn't home I took the girls down with me, not really entertaining any hopes that I could play, but just to take the men my share of the music…we stayed and listened to them playing, and the girls were very charming (Heidi *wouldn't* have been charming if I had neglected her for a fiddle!) and shook hands very precisely and correctly with Tirzah and were very quiet during the music. I was glad to take the opportunity to introduce them to a home which is so patently not designed for children (visiting or otherwise) and to let them realize that certain elegancies are Not To Be Touched…even Heidi viewed the Steuben crystal ashtrays with the proper gravity and didn't attempt to touch one of them. All in all, the visit was a great success, and Tirzah begged me to bring them again.

June 1955

Sam is all enthusiastic about skin-diving now, and has conveyed it irrevocably to a few of his friends, David Tolerton and Walter Trotter and Emile. Now they come up and practice with their snorkels in the pool; as soon as the ocean calms somewhat (my, it has been savagely rough lately!) they are all going to different local beaches and locate the abalone. Sam went out in Partington Cove last week and brought back stories of an incredible new world under there, with strange tiny gleaming fish and huge anemones and iridescent jelly fish and such…just the plant life alone must be incredible…I long to see it all.

*　*　*

The weather has been so hot and dry here that I fear our berry crop will be negligible…so disappointing. Sam tells me to look on the bright side of being saved all the work of jam-making and pie-making, etc. But I still feel crushed about it all. In the next few weeks we'll get lugs of fruit in town and I'll can and freeze it…our peach trees are loaded with fruit, and if I beat the blue jays to it we ought to have a good crop of these. Believe me, you battle for a garden here in the wilds!

July 1955

Our cocktail party for neighbors on Monday evening was a big success…beautiful warm weather and the food was very good and plenteous…I was a little dubious about the amounts, for I have never served dinner to such a crowd…we had a 22-pound ham and only a little bit left afterward. Sam took charge of the bar…set up a liquor table out on the porch with great tubs of ice and such. I had fixed a picnic supper for the seven children to eat out under the oak tree, and afterwards they all went swimming…we put the spotlight on the pool so we could count heads occasionally…they were in seventh heaven, all shouting and splashing.

*　*　*

Sam's half of the garden looks magnificent…we have been eating string beans and broccoli and zucchini, and the tomatoes and corn are almost ripe, but *my* half is quite frowzy and unpresentable…the lettuce and onions are the only things that can be considered a success. I do grow magnificent earwigs, however…super huge, fat, succulent ones.

Nan tending the garden

We are laying plans to put in a really well-laid-out berry patch between the vegetable garden and the chicken house next winter. Of course, like all of our plans, this projected berry-patch may not materialize. We are all too apt to lay plans for improvements but then never summon up the energy to carry them into effect (by "we" of course I mean Lazy Sam and Lazy Nancy and not just a general "we"). Of course, to balance the scales, it must be admitted that we have lots of *fun*, which is every bit as good as being married to projects…this time of year we feel that picnics and skin-diving and surf-swimming are just More Fun Than Any Tilling Of The Soil!

Five

"There is so much to do."

With the birth of her fourth child, Chris, Nan had her hands full. It was still a year before the oldest would enter school, there being no preschool or kindergarten in Big Sur, so all four were at home. Life was increasingly hectic. Sam pitched in, but he also found more reasons to be away on hikes with friends into the backcountry and on hunts in Nevada instead of in the brushy draws close to home. The tenor of Nan's letters during this period reflects her exhaustion and a wistful yearning for travel.

This same year—1955—Giles and Sheila Healey, with a baby girl my age, bought Frank Trotter's former home and became our "next-door neighbors" (a good half-mile away). This gave me the opportunity, as I grew up, to regularly and spontaneously enjoy friendship with someone outside the family. None of my siblings enjoyed this advantage.

September 1955

We have had great heat since you left…we had up to 98 degrees, and of course the heat doesn't abate here at night. Poor little Chris was very rashy indeed…just one continuous blotch from head to foot. Now we are back to a peak of 90 degrees, which seems deliciously cool, and Chris is back to his pink-and-white norm.

We took a day at the beach during the worst of the heat and had a lovely time…we somehow collected Richard Trotter (who is 10) along the way. Jory and Darien managed to keep up with him, and as the three of them raced miles up the beach and disappeared around rocky outcroppings I just put my faith in something-or-other and trusted that somehow I would see them again. You can't *quite* rely on a ten-year-old to keep a three-year-old safe, but I was stuck in one place by Chris and Heidi, and Sam was spearfishing out in the water.

Cal came up to see us last night, out of the mountains to get supplies and new shoes for his horses. He had horrendous tales to tell of the heat back there and the pestilential swarms of yellow jackets (which we have also had here to a lesser degree) and the utter misery of it all. How we have escaped fires so far in this country amazes us…the fire danger has never been so extreme. All of the local Forest Service men except Cal are away on fires in other parts of the state, so if anything happens here we shall be sadly undermanned.

Hiking above the Molera Ranch

* * *

Both of the older girls are wonderful little walkers. Since Chris arrived I haven't been able to get too far from the house, but Sam takes them for long walks in the hills almost every day, either in the early morning or the evening. They go for great distances and think nothing of really steep country, for he is careful *not* to keep them on trails. Lately they have been bringing back from these treks great armfuls of pearly everlasting and golden maple leaves, which tells me that fall is really here.

Summer was hot here…the hottest we remember…the fruit flourished, all except the berries which like it cooler and moister. Now we have great heavy bunches of grapes hanging from the vines…I munch on the blue-black Concords all afternoon, and summer itself seems to be distilled in the winy juice of each grape. The figs are fat and black, too, and dropping into the girls' sand pile below…Heidi likes a judicious mixture of fig and sand. But the air has become crisper in the last few days, the sea of fog below us has risen and we watch it sifting among the branches of the redwood trees only five hundred or so feet below our ridge, and it cools the air. Great cumulus clouds have begun to form behind the high ridge above our home, and there are vague, undefined rustlings in the pine trees…sure signs of autumn.

* * *

I am busy with the household, certainly; we shall keep our life very quiet this winter, for it is really impossible to do otherwise. Fortunately there are so many of us at the table now that every night ends up a party! Last night I presented the family with my first pumpkin pie…a great dazzling experiment…Sam rewarded me by saying that, without any qualification, it was the best pumpkin pie he had ever eaten and that I must never vary the recipe *one iota*. It *was* good. Now I feel ready for all the years of Thanksgivings ahead.

* * *

Last weekend we all got together and had a house-raising for Harry Dick, to get a small rental house weather-proof before the rains. About 18 men came to help him on both Saturday and Sunday, and the wives brought food for the midday meal—great steaming kettles of Spanish beans and golden fried chicken and mountains of potato salad and enormous bowls of green salad and the pies and cakes that Big Sur women are famous for. It was such wonderful fun. Of course there were great tubs full of ice, piled with beer bottles, and *that* seemed to help the work along. Great joking went on and many a prank was played, for everyone was in the best of spirits. Of course, as at any coast event, there were the usual children scampering about. In spite of it all, the roof and walls were all finished…now Harry Dick just has to put the finishing touches on the inside. It will give him a nice little monthly income, which he needs for Shanagolden has not been well and he had to give up his job bartending at Nepenthe so as to be home with her.

[Note: Shanagolden suffered from dementia, perhaps Alzheimer's.]

[Sam's rainfall record]

		Hottest summer we remember. Many nights 84 all night. 98 on porch. No fog up here at all in July and Aug. Chris born Aug. 15.
Nov. 13	1.00"	*A long dry summer. Autumn pleasant but no rain. Low barometers. Used 7-06 this season—9 bucks locally, 3 in Nevada. Too many.*

Power Outages

P ower outages are a way of life in Big Sur. No technological advance has overcome the sheer adversity of Big Sur's rugged terrain. Landslides, flailing branches and trees falling under hurricane-velocity south winds all can bring down power poles and lines. Compounding the problem, it takes an hour or more for the utility services, which are based on the Monterey Peninsula, to get down the coast, and, with the Big Sur coast's low population density, a downed line along the coast can take a backseat to problems in more populated areas.

On the positive side, the frequency of power outages means that people are set up to live without power. When the lights flicker out, residents get out their candles and kerosene or propane lamps, fire up generators, and continue with their daily business.

November 1955

The first real rain of the season has descended upon us, and we are enjoying it thoroughly. Of course the electricity has gone off (it always does during the first storm) but fortunately it allowed me to get the laundry done and custard and cookies baked before giving up the ghost. Now we gleefully plan to roast a hunk of lamb in the fireplace for dinner, which will make us feel quite like a tribe of Bedouins or a cave-full of Sicilian banditti, and with a musty bottle of wine to wash it down it shouldn't be bad at all. It is fun to get out the old faithful Aladdin lamps...*they* never fail us.

Sam will walk down the road this afternoon to see that the culverts are open and of course will end up at the Rosses to celebrate the first rain with a toast.

Now it is snowing on the ridge above us (as we saw when the clouds lifted for a few minutes). Just yesterday we were at the beach for the day, which shows how rapidly the weather can change this time of year.

* * *

Skin-diving has taken the "old coast" group by storm, for abaloneing has always been a traditional coast activity for the ranch families, and wearing the rubber suits and swimming out into fairly deep water has made it possible for them to get the huge abalone that are so impossible to find right along the shore rocks. So now all the ranch men are getting the suits…and by the time the Trotters and the Posts and the Danis bring along their kids and womenfolk we are *really* a large group.

A day at the beach

Christmas Note from Nan

Oh Nick…and Tirzah, better half…
Run and kill the fatted calf;
Haste and fill the bowl of cheer;
Saturday at last is here.
Musicians stream in at the door,
(Never, never less than four),
Come from haunts of coot or tern,
But one and all, for food they yearn.
They'll draw a bow, or strum the keys,
Or sight-read Beethoven with ease,
Or tackle Brandenburgs, but gracious,
Truth to tell, they're all voracious.
When kitchen sounds are heard at last
Their eyes light up, their hearts beat fast.
When groaning board before them lies
They rush pell-mell to gourmandize.

Austere disciple of bohea,
Our gentle Gene he sippeth tea,
Ever polished, suave, and urban.
Charlie headeth for the bourbon,
Nor calleth halt to one more drynke
'Til bourbon be all gone, I thynke.
The sober flautist waxeth frisky,

Thanks to Nick's imported whiskey.
Nan cavorteth with bravado,
Lapping up Amontillado.
As for the knavish others, some
Are known to lace their tea with rum,
With fingers crookt all mannerly…
Deplorable hypocrisy.

As ocean surges in to shore
So greedy fiddlers dive for more;
Peacocks' tongues and truffles rare
Disappear into thin air.
Fast as Tirzah can replenish
Heaping bowls, it all doth vanish.
At length, when surfeit is in store,
They reel and totter to the door
To wend their way to distant dells
And, unrepentant, say farewells.
(L'envoi) Oh worthy Nick and Tirzah dear,
Take now my offering of good cheer.
And may this pint of nut-brown sherrye
Make your new year hale and merrye.

Merry Christmas from Sam and Nancy

Yesterday we went down the coast to our favorite abalone spot north of San Simeon…it is a weekend event now and a huge crowd turns out. There were about 18 grownups yesterday and about the same number of children of all ages, plus about six large rambunctious ranch dogs… really a brawl. We had all brought different parts of the noon meal, and roasted wienies and enjoyed great bowlfuls of salad and panfuls of cake and such. It was a heavenly hot blue day…the ocean was windless and as calm as glass, and the tide was very low. The children had a most marvelous time racing through the water and collecting all sorts of small sea life from the tide pools. The men came to shore with great loads of abalone and also some huge purple sea-urchins which a few of them proceeded to eat raw…they claim it is a rare delicacy. The children and I were rock-hunting down the beach and so didn't get a taste of the urchins…there were none left when we returned.

Farewell for now, for I have to pound the abalone we brought home yesterday…my chore, and a very time-consuming one.

December 1955

By evening I find it rather an effort to take up the fiddle. I think it isn't so much that I am physically tired, but after dealing with a sea of life from dawn to 8 o'clock I find it sweeter to spend the evening quietly repairing my own inner resources by reading…I do need at least an hour or two every day to retreat into myself!

* * *

We are in the midst of a big storm, or perhaps rather a series of them…such fun. We are all holed in and all hell is breaking loose outside. Intently as we study meteorology we never shall be able to fathom the elements…just as we think we have the weather patterns all figured out everything changes. Everyone knows that storms move in on a falling barometer, and yet this winter every rain has come on a high barometer…today it is sky high and yet gale winds are blowing from the south and the rain is heavy. So what does it all mean? In summer a low barometer means that the coastal fog will rise and engulf us, and yet all summer we had the lowest barometer ever and never a day of fog until the end of October. This year is bewitched.

* * *

Mr. Owings (the architect of Skidmore, Owings and Merrill) is finally building his house here on the coast…right plunk on the tip of Grimes Point which is nothing but sheer rocky cliff plunging 700 feet to the ocean…the building area is literally smaller than our living-room rug, but he plans to cantilever out over space on both sides which will end up with rather an airborne feeling…you will glance out the window and see nothing but air and sea lions 700 feet below…the idea doesn't appeal too much to me, but for an architect's showplace (really just a weekend retreat) I suppose it has its points. An all-local crew is doing all the preliminary work, and then Granite Construction will build the house itself. Sam has been working there a few days a week, suspended on the cliff by a rope while he puts expansion bolts in the rock. You can imagine how he loves that, and of course no one else could be persuaded to do it at all!

* * *

Sam was doing odd jobs indoors today, and had the "full treatment" from Heidi; he was exhausted by lunchtime and seemed ready for something drastic like the shock treatment or at least a lobotomy. To me he said, "How do you stand her *all day long?*" It made me roar with laughter. I was so glad that at last his eyes were opened to what goes on around here. Oh, what an age! Such shenanigans, such reckless and extensive mayhem, such absolute absence of any sense of right and wrong, such imperviousness to any sense of reason and order. We decided humorously over lunch (Heidi's exuberant spirits making a fiasco of that once-serene interlude) that one should only be with a 19-month-old for ten minutes a day…in that way one could still

Ashley Justice ("Sandy")

"Sandy knows a hawk from a handsaw when the wind is southerly," wrote Nan, "but he spends all too many of his leisure moments discriminating a Chianti from a Valpolicella."

One of Big Sur's many extraordinary characters, Southern gentleman Ashley Justice—locally known as Sandy—lived as our neighbor at the Angulo ranch in the years after linguist Jaime de Angulo had died. While less flamboyant than Jaime, Sandy carried on Jaime's tradition of drunkenness and abandon in his own fashion. The gallon jug of Red Mountain wine was always on hand as was the large tin of tobacco for rolling cigarettes. Long dead cars and trucks accumulated on the property. Once in a generous fit Sandy acquired 50 toilets and 25 sinks from a business that was disposing of them with the idea that he could give them out to his friends. For some years they lined the road into the ranch, and ultimately many of them ended up shoring up an eroding gully.

When Mrs. Angulo sold the ranch in the 1980s, Sandy was last seen heading off to Nevada in a stately caravan of old cars, pickups, a fire engine and a city transit bus, which had a horse, a cow and several goats peering bemusedly out the windows.

find them charming. As I carried her off for her nap she gave us all her sweetest smile (and there never was a smile like Heidi's!) and kissed her chubby little hands at us and I had to say "But she is *so* adorable" and Sam said wryly "especially when she is receding into the distance."

January 1956

If I started to tell you about this Christmas on the coast, it would take me a week, so I shall only summarize with headlines. Great rain. More rain to date than *all* of last year. Roads out everywhere. Highway completely washed away a mile south of Partington, cutting off many families. Everybody's cars caught in mudslides on highway. Cars washed out to ocean. A baby packed in knapsack, rushed to town with pneumonia…safe now, thank Heaven. Lower Partington without water for 10 days. Electricity out for one day (Christmas). Beautiful hail and snow last Friday. Tolerton's house struck by lightning…great havoc. Betty stunned, but okay now.

* * *

[letter from Sam]

We have had a stormy Yuletide to put it mildly. In fact we have not seen the sun for 10 days. Two of the series of storms to hit us were extra violent with high winds and heavy rain. Last Thursday night for example we had 9.1 inches of rain in 12 hours. The most I had ever previously recorded was 6 inches in 24 hours. So you can imagine what our road is like. Most of the culverts stopped up the night of the downpour in spite of my efforts, and as a consequence there are slides and wash-outs. But we have come through it pretty well. Nancy and I really got quite a kick out of the whole thing; particularly the moans and groans of our less venturesome neighbors. Great parties and social activities were planned on the lower ridge for Xmas. Of course everything had to be cancelled. The road slid in, the lights went out and to cap it all, the Partington pipeline was wrecked…slides have broken the pipe in two places. One, a 60-foot section, was washed into the canyon and twisted like spaghetti. So they are running around with pots and pans trying to save rain water.

* * *

Our fabulous bearded neighbor Sandy went off the road again last week in his huge truck and once again a providentially-placed oak tree saved him from going to Kingdom Come…some Omnipotent Force is very anxious to keep him among the living. Everyone on the lower ridge feels that this is the last straw and they are racking their brains to think of a way to remove him from the locale…he *is* a menace on the road, no doubt about it, for none of his assorted vehicles have any brakes worth speaking of; but I suppose we worry less about it than the other people because we don't actually use the road too often and so feel that our chances of meeting him on it are rather less than other people's.

Actually we can't help but be very fond of Sandy in a way…he has some delightful quali-
ties which make up for the facts that he is an alcoholic and dishonest; knowing him is a
liberal education in a new approach to humanity. If you condemn us for admitting to an
affection for such a man, we are perhaps saved by the fact that both the Phelps (than whom
there can be no one more upright and gentle and respectable) are also very fond of him and
see great things in him. He probably comes very close to being a Falstaff type…hardly of "good
character" but one's neck would have to be very stiff indeed for one not to like him.

* * *

I suppose it is just as well that you didn't plan a visit this week, for we are having great rains
again…three inches last night (which isn't heavy for here, but a good steady rain). We really
have enjoyed this winter…somehow we had anticipated it being difficult, with the four children
so small, but it has been lots of fun and they have adjusted beautifully to indoor life. Jory and
Darien play out on the porches when they want to run and chase, and they have high boots so
they can rush outdoors and splash through the puddles between downpours. Indoors they cut
out pictures and make scrapbooks and draw with crayons and read books and dress up for all
sorts of imaginative games…Heidi joins in some of them, but plays alone too a great deal of the
time. She is the first of our brood to manifest a real need for being alone part of each day…both
the other girls definitely prefer company if it is to be had. But Heidi will come and ask me if
she can go into her room and play by herself in the crib…and off she trots with a stack of books
in her chubby little arms and will read by herself in the crib for an hour or two. Sam and I are
very sympathetic toward this need, for we are both lovers of solitude too.

* * *

Our road is in the most marvelous state of mud and disrepair. Sandy, our neighbor, has all
his various trucks stranded along it at various points, and often they are exactly placed so that
it is impossible for anyone else to get by. Yesterday afternoon I went down to Nick's to play
music and had to park the jeep at Stephens Flat (just above the old Partington House) and walk
down from there with my fiddles, for there were two trucks nosed together at that spot. Good
old Sandy! On my way home I ran into him with his buddy Sean walking up the hill to the
ranch and I gave them a lift. That pair has to be seen to be believed…bearded, absolutely
disreputable-looking, lugging gunny sacks of goodness knows what and also a gallon jug of
wine. I asked them jokingly how they could carry such a heavy wine jug and Sandy said, "That's
what gets us up the hill." Sean remarked that they "lighten it as they go along and by the time
they get home it is very light indeed, being all air." They really are a pair…quite a frightening
apparition in those lonely woods for anyone who didn't know them. But Sam and I know they are
harmless and are always glad to give them a lift. Sandy was very appealing, for he was trying so hard

to seem sober. I think he felt that I would be somehow offended at his drunkenness and I was very touched by his wanting to retain my good opinion…it showed me better than anything he has ever done that he is fond of me and anxious to please me, for he is famous for being very devil-may-care when he is drunk and can get quite abusive with people that he doesn't like when his inhibitions are relaxed. Poor fellow…that is a terrible flaw to have. But those of us who get to know him cannot but be fond of him…he is very gentlemanly in his way.

* * *

On his way up to the boys' home yesterday Sam stopped in at Walter Trotter's home for a minute…found Walter's six-year-old son Mike there and asked him why he wasn't in school…Mike said dourly, "I have to go in to the goddam dentist and I hate it," not, he went on to say in his own particular vernacular, because of the pain but because of "all the little brats bawlin' around and it don't even hurt much!" In spite of his lack of grammar and urban politeness (which amused Sam greatly), Mike is a marvelous child. He fairly bursts with the manly virtues of bravery and stoicism, very dear to behold, especially in a boy. Not long ago he fell off a roof that his father was working on and laid a huge wound open above his eye…he didn't cry a bit, just shouted up to Walter, "I can't see, Daddy" and there he was all drenched in blood. Walter rushed him in to the hospital for stitches, which he had with no anesthetic and didn't whimper once. And last year when he was five he remarked at the supper table that he had killed a rattlesnake that afternoon…no one of course believed him; they assumed that he had killed a garter-snake or something. But later his older brother Sammy went out in the yard and found a huge rattler which Mike had killed and then neatly dismembered in two-inch segments with a little hatchet to make sure that it was "really dead."

I do like manliness in boys….

* * *

The garden promises to sprout soon…oh, woe. I haven't yet summoned up courage to venture out in the cold air to cut off the old stalks, and here we have new ones shooting up. A few golden spring days will change my attitude, of course; but by then it will be very hard to sort out the old stalks from the new. But if that is the greatest of my woes this year I shan't complain!

February 1956

The winter has been lovely here…raging storms and then stretches of clear blue days, sometimes with huge cloud masses banked against the ridge above our home. The air seems to be always in movement…not windy and yet not the absolute stillness that makes summer such a breathless, dreamlike time. Our road, alas, practically gave up the ghost during the December storm. It is passable, but *just.* If at all wet it is only passable by jeep. This spring we shall have to do something drastic, but it seems folly to attempt any repairs until dry weather is definitely here to stay. The first pepperroot has appeared in the woods, a charming harbinger of bright carpets to come.

* * *

On our way home from town yesterday we picked up Sam and the older girls at Post's. They had walked there from home…a good ten-mile hike, which is a good distance for a four- and six-year-old. The girls weren't tired at all…they were scampering all over Post's with some other children when we got there and that evening they stayed up until nine with no signs of fatigue at all. Sam had carried their little sleeping bags with him, and they both took naps after lunch. I suspect that by the time they are eight and ten they will be the talk of the coast…wonderful little walkers.

* * *

I have the "going" bug after these almost-six months of quite thorough and constant house-wifery. Emile made the mistake the other night of suggesting that he and Sam and I fly to the Bahamas sometime in the not too distant future and spend a few weeks skin-diving and collecting shells. "I'm ready," I said. "Right now. This Minute. Just let me get a suitcase." We finally decided that various reasons made it imperative for us to wait for a day or two…Emile's contract with the Masons, an unweaned baby, flat wallets. But it was a lovely thought…We have promised ourselves that we Positively Shall before we die.

* * *

On Saturdays I luxuriate in the radio broadcasts of the Metropolitan opera; armed with libretti I cast all else to the winds. When Sam comes into the house he either hums passionately "Cherchez la femme, cherchez la femme" (if it is a French opera) or sobs woefully "addio, addio, addio" (if it is an Italian opera) or snorts raucously "Ho-yo-to-ho-YOH!" (if it is Wagner). He insists that these three phrases can sum up the three categories and that all the rest of the libretto is superfluous. He is quite wrong. Actually, he puts up with my love of opera very manfully. He has even suggested posting a sign every Saturday at the bottom of our road saying, "Today is Saturday. Approach at your own risk," for it ruins my entire day to have callers drop in and I put a very glum face forward.

I can still remember the first opera I ever saw…it was *Traviata* and I was fifteen or sixteen and I wept all the way through it and felt as though the gates of Paradise had been opened and that I had seen true beauty for the first time…I hadn't believed that anything so angelically ravishing could possibly exist. Of course, I am no longer sixteen and, as Wordsworth has said, we get further from these ecstatic experiences…but one still glimpses them, and I cannot believe that anything which can do this to a human consciousness can be completely worthless.

Sam kayaking on a calm day

March 1956

Last week Sam took the kayak out on the ocean and returned with FIFTY pounds of fish, which is now all nicely filleted and stored in the freezer. He also returned with a glowing account of a great whale that rose out of the water near him on its migration north; it was so close that it looked like a freight car and he could count the barnacles on its back, and he had a few moments' apprehension that it might be traveling with a mate that might rise beneath him and upset the kayak…and our coast water is so cold that only ten minutes in it are enough to immobilize one.

* * *

I am a great lover of travel (not that I do much now, but everything in its time), and much more so now than ten years ago just because at last I really feel at home in the world. But now of course is the time for the raising of the young. So I travel by the fireside, and that is good, too…almost the same adventure. Sam and I have great fun with atlases. We get out maps after breakfast on rainy days and really gloat over the possibilities.

Last Wednesday night we practically packed our bags and headed for the Windward Isles, for Clem had seen an advertisement for an island for sale in that group (part of the Lesser Antilles, off the coast of Venezuela…British West Indies) and it sounded so wonderful. And we had been rather depressed thinking that a population of 300 from Gorda to Carmel Highlands to be just a bit Too Much. But an *island*…10,000 arable acres and more wild land, three houses…one for us, one for the boys, one for an exciting unknown quantity…it sounded so perfect. The Windward Isles. Isn't it lovely? Clem could have his boat, which he so longs for.

Emile and Sam could dive for oysters and flying fish. I could till the 10,000 arable acres. After all, why not? Why California? When too many people come here, away go we.

[Sam's rainfall record]

Apr. 1	*.25"*	*One of the toughest winters yet. First a deluge then a drought. Feed very poor.*
Apr. 9	*.40"*	
Apr. 10	*1.60"*	*Thank God! Maybe some of the grass will be saved.*
Apr. 11	*.25"*	
Apr. 26	*1.25"*	
Apr. 27	*.65"*	
May 4	*1.30"*	*These late rains are wonderful! Most of the grass revived. The flowers are fine. Am looking forward to beautiful godetias.*

April 1956

You said a very wise thing in one of your letters. "There is so much to do." I say it to myself very solemnly almost every day, but it really affords little comfort. When I add up the projects on my mind, the view seems very dismal indeed. I wish sometimes that we mothers had nothing to do but guide the children through a creative day. Jory has such an exciting project under way, and I so long to spend time with her on it; she is laying out a miniature ranch down under the fig tree…so far she has a ranch house and a barn and a haystack and a corral and a road and a place where she wants a river to go (two small plastic beavers wait there hopefully). But we could go on so far from there, with silos and perhaps a pond and even a field with real crops growing…grass seed could make a marvelous corn field. But as soon as we get really absorbed in it, it is time to sort the laundry or patch the blue jeans or scrub milk off the rug.

May 1956

Last weekend we managed to get the children all parked out one place or another and Sam and I climbed Pico Blanco. We camped Saturday night near the foot of the mountain, after a several-hour hike in. It was a beautiful clear weekend, with the grass still green and lovely; it was a steep 2,300-foot climb to the peak, which is solid dazzling limestone near the top. And we had a most magnificent view of the watersheds of the two forks of the Little Sur River which circle the peak except for one small saddle; it is a monadnock technically; it stands apart from the rest of the range. A lovely weekend. The vegetation down along the Little Sur River is tropical in its lushness…enormous ferns everywhere and spilling waterfalls and carpets of oxalis and yellow violets in bloom…a shady wonderland.

* * *

Tomorrow I go to play music at Nick's (for the first Saturday in a month or two) and on Sunday afternoon we are going up to the Lyon's hilltop for what Terre and Jimmie call a "bash"…all the two Trotter families will be there, and the Ewoldsens and Clem and Emile, and drinking will start at two and Terre says that if she isn't too drunk there will be food at 4. With five of Frank's youngsters and three of Walter's and small Matt Lyons (5 months) and our own, there ought to be enough small fry to make the welkin ring.

Jimmie is a disc jockey in Monterey…his great interest (beside the country here) is jazz…consequently his and Terre's conversation is always spiced with the latest phrases from the jazz world. They are lots of fun to be with, even if we don't agree with them about the importance of jive. They can't "dig" Bach and Beethoven…as Terre says, "there's no beat."

* * *

We do look forward to summer…it is a time of year when time seems to stand still here, and of course the youngsters have such a glorious time racing around barefooted and clad only in shorts. And we love barbequing and having our meals out on the big screen porch; the mornings are so delicious that Sam grumbles that I never get up from the breakfast table from June to October.

The screen porch in the late afternoon

June 1956

On Wednesday was the school play-day, and the Hopkins migrated en masse to the all-day event, with a potluck lunch and all sorts of games and folk-dances and the graduation exercises (one girl graduated from Pfeiffer School). These events are landmarks...everyone comes, including fathers and interested friends who enjoy a mass picnic. Sam brought a jug of wine and was the center of a small but assiduous group, for no one else had thought to bring the fruit of the vine.

In spite of all the end-of-school activity I did get lots done, for I made a list on Saturday morning of Things that I Positively Would Get Done that weekend. It was a formidable list indeed, and I did *everything* on it. And everything was done by noon on Sunday, so I felt very noble and virtuous and spent the afternoon catching butterflies with the girls.

* * *

Are you really as "busy" as your letters reiterate? It exhausts me just to think about it! Sometimes I suspect that your generation was raised and firmly implanted with the idea that to be "busy" is to be virtuous. How odd. We Hopkins cannot at all agree with that conception of virtue; just the other day an English writer put our philosophy into print...she writes, "I have been taking stock ruthlessly, as one does now and again, and I find that I work much harder than I need, which is stupid. There is a school of morality that considers things like hard work and getting up early in the morning as virtuous in themselves. But what nonsense. It is only inefficient not to arrange one's affairs to have time for a civilized life." That is, quite baldly, the way we feel too.

July 1956

A cold Sunday with sick children is conducive to some things; I made two skirts for Jory and Darien which look adorable on them and which please them immensely. Today I did a massive laundry, scrubbed up a bed, transplanted small lettuces and sweet Williams, viewed the garden with rage, indignation, disappointment, etc. When I close this letter I shall attack a dirty bathtub, vacuum the house, pick raspberries, and in general have everything shipshape when Sam comes home so that he can harbor the illusion that "all is under control" on the home front (this "illusion" is a family jest...we all know that nothing is under control but we try to pretend en masse that it is).

Not long ago *Life* magazine had a spread on a typical day of a young Seattle mother with three small boys...she gave a wonderful answer to one of their questions that seemed to me to sum up our period of motherhood perfectly. They asked her how she plans her day's work and she said, "I don't really plan it...I just plunge in and do what I can."

"Oh sweet, loved, naughty, obstreperous Christopher!"

August 1956

Chris has turned one. He charges around like a small steam engine these days, with his chubby little arms held in the air to steady himself. He is dreadfully adventurous and loves to be outdoors; he can open the screen doors by himself (occasionally he gets pinched) and disappears in no time. Yesterday he fell off a four-foot wall onto the lawn; frequently he gets snagged by mouse traps; today he picked up a bee but miraculously wasn't stung.

It is as though already Chris has identified himself with the world of men. He is in seventh heaven if a cement mixer is in action or a tractor is pushing out a bank. He can open door knobs, uncap bottles, remove lampshades, shift gears on the car (he is a real menace to drive with). And his two words are "daddy" and "gun"…isn't it appalling?

I'll stop this rambling and get out the sewing machine…for when Chris awakes from his nap it will be very difficult to get the sewing worked on; everything gets pulled off the table and onto the floor and it becomes a desperate struggle to keep him from swallowing pins and needles and tossing pattern papers into the fireplace. Oh sweet, loved, naughty, obstreperous Christopher!

Six

"I shall point at my children frolicking on the lawn and say,
'There are my flowers.'"

The Big Sur school in 1956 was a one-room school. To accommodate increased enroll-ment, the first three grades shared the school's small supply room while the five upper grades shared the main classroom. There was no preschool or kindergarten.

Getting to school was a challenge. A school bus operated along Highway 1, but getting down to the bus took some doing, particularly in the winter when nighttime downpours could leave the dirt road blocked by a rock slide or a fallen oak. While our parents did lots of ferrying back and forth to the bus, often in coordination with neighbors, the ridge chil-dren also were expected to walk. With no phone service, all these arrangements were made more difficult; when the phones arrived in 1958, some complications eased.

To this day, the sound of rain on the roof triggers a sense of bliss. When we woke to rain drumming on the roof in those early school years, it usually meant that our parents would forgo the trip down the hill, and Nan would instruct us at home. I'm sure Nan was diligent in getting us to do our schoolwork, but all I remember about those blissful days were the "recesses" when we ran outside to play in the puddles and the delights of tea-and-cinnamon-toast by the fire in the afternoon.

September 1956

Jory is loving school, after a few days of being very worried about it. She has talked about wanting to go to school for several years now, but when it came to the actual thing she was very nervous and anxious about it (the daughter of her parents!)…she upchucked her tomato juice and then asked if she could skip breakfast. So I let her just nibble a piece of raisin toast, and off she went with Sam to meet the bus. The next day she seemed much more cheerful, and today she was positively high-spirited at the breakfast table. So all is well, and I know she is having lots of fun. Unfortunately, she is the only girl in the first three grades (there are eight boys). The teacher tells me that she is going to organize circle games and such at the recess time and that will ensure Jory's not being left out as a "mere smear girl."

She has a fiendishly long day…she leaves home at 7:30 and isn't home until 5 or so, which is quite an ordeal for a 6-year-old. Fortunately the teacher understands; Jory fell asleep at her desk one afternoon and she just let her nap there for an hour.

This letter must cease for it is already two o'clock, and I have to feed Chris, clean out the icebox, fold and put away laundry, get some things organized for dinner, and brace myself for a strenuous hour of kickball at four, for I have promised Jory that everything will be in order by then so that I can practice playing ball with her. She is most eager to master the occult arts of volleyball and kickball, and she practices faithfully.

*　*　*

Somehow the beginning of school marks the beginning of such a new era in family life. Most of our thoughts are directed toward the education of the children…how we can best fulfill the potentials of their minds. Reading magazines and newspapers lately I have been even more aware of how the next generation is going to have to use every ounce of mind and sense of values that they have available; the scientists are just beginning to have an inkling of what terrible things can come if we continue creating radioactivity by our bomb tests. Isn't it frightening? And yet so many people who are in positions of responsibility have no real sense of the gravity of their decisions and the splendor of man's heritage.

[Nan's entries in Sam's rainfall record]

> Oct. 1　*Sam left for Canada with Keith.*
>
> Oct. 2　*Light sprinkle of rain.*
>
> Oct. 3　*Sudden hard downpour with thunder and lightning.*
> *Wish Sam were here.*

November 1956

We are having lovely weather here this weekend, after a fine rain earlier in the week. The summer's dust is all gone from the road and trees, and now perhaps things will start to turn green. We survey the garden with satisfaction, for now we don't have to do anything until April or so. I still pick a few tomatoes, enough for our own needs and some to give away. And there will be broccoli and cabbage, both red and green, for a couple of months to come. But everything just sits, including the weeds, and that is just the way we like it. The grape leaves are dropping, and the fruit tree leaves are turning yellow.

*　*　*

Your last letter amused us vastly. You have this marvelous picture built up in your mind of Sam slaving single-mindedly at building a house, with nary a moment off for such wickedness as Idleness; Sam isn't Daddy! The new room progresses, but only by fits and starts. Many things intervene, either in Sam's life or in Walter's. Walter may show up to work, and he may not, and we never know, which lends a delicious uncertainty to the whole thing. Sam says that he is probably the only man in the world who is delighted when the workmen *don't* show up for work. Because then Sam can renege too. Big Sur does go at such a splendidly slow pace. Things that matter a great deal elsewhere don't seem to matter at all here.

On New Year's Day it seemed as though a hundred people came calling, but they were all our favorite people so it was lots of fun. And on January 2 we took down our decorations and managed to set the chimney on fire…I thought it couldn't hurt to toss the mistletoe on the fire as a sort of poetic symbol of love enveloping our hearth in the coming year. It enveloped us, all right…whoosh! But we have become quite a good family team in meeting disaster and got the fire out quickly. The girls show very good sense in these matters…they don't go to pieces or anything. I think they will all be very sensible people, which is a blessing.

* * *

Certainly the home will always be a most crucial training ground. Sam and I have been giving this all tremendous thought lately, as we watch Jory moving on her own in the world outside the home. She reacts almost completely as the home has prepared her to react; it is really so very encouraging. Her sense of right and wrong, of fairness and good sportsmanship, prevail even when she sees violations of these ideals all around her; once in a while she gets puzzled and timidly brings up situations that she hasn't quite understood, but most of the time she prefers to steer her own course and make her own decisions. And from what I sense of those decisions, they seem to be very sound.

* * *

I wish you could see the white world we are living in. It snowed all last night and there is at least four inches of snow on the ground and the sky still white and mobile with the silently falling flakes. The barometer is still falling, so we ought to be in for a great deal more…Sam predicts a foot or two of snow before the skies clear.

Today was Darien's birthday, and she considers that Nature sent this great gift just for her. She spent all morning outdoors, in boots and slicker and woolen cap and mittens, making snowmen and pelting our windows with snowballs. I made her come in to warm up by the fire, and her cheeks and nose looked like three little cherries.

The birthday was a great success, though the neighbors couldn't get up the hill for our dinner party, even in their jeep. The road was a foot deep in snow, which froze over in an icy surface. Jory walked the mile home from their house late in the afternoon, amid a small blizzard. God bless our rugged little mountain girls!

Fun in the snow

* * *

The girls have taken over all the dish wiping, and Sam is amazed (and delighted) that he can sit down after dinner with a book and a pipe by the fireplace while his daughters fly at the clean-up job. "This is living," he says.

February 1957

Great havoc happened to everyone during a terrible deluge and windstorm the night before last, and yesterday and today everyone is helping everyone else to repair damages. The worst catastrophe was that one neighbor's roofing blew off completely, leaving the pouring rain to come through the planks of the roof and fairly well ruin her books, walls, upholstery, furniture, etc. Because this all happened late at night she couldn't get anyone to help her. Yesterday afternoon the men hastily nailed on more roofing for her (in the rain).

* * *

Jory does very well in music, and loves it. She is one of nine children chosen to sing in a chorus at the county school music festival in April. Gene is a wonderful teacher for the children; he is kind and patient and they all adore him, and also has that marvelous quality of perfect taste in his choice of music…he doesn't have them singing the current radio tunes or anything "ordinary"; the chorus is working on a charming little Spanish love song, and also a very early fugue. The music he chooses for the Christmas pageants is always superlative…the little heard but especially lovely carols from various countries…never the banal.

* * *

[Sam's rainfall record]

Apr. 14	1.25"	*Almost too late.*
Apr. 18	2.80"	*Thunderstorm. Heavy rain. Always after I scrape road.*
Apr. 22	.80"	*Snow!*
May 3	1.00"	*Beautiful grass.*
May 6	.55"	
May 11	1.75"	*Fantastic weather. A little rain almost every day.*
May 13	.45"	*Every day.*
May 18	3.85"	*Amazing, unheard of.*
May 18	1.35"	*Revolutionary!*

* * *

We are having such a late, wet spring. Our last day of sunshine was two weeks ago on May 4, and we had nothing but fog and rain since. On last Saturday we had five and a half inches of rain, which for this country is unheard of after the end of March. Of course the hills are gloriously green, and the foliage lush, but the wetness prevents us from getting out to enjoy the bright yucca blooms and other wildflowers.

* * *

This last month I have been in a revel of reading; I go so erratically from periods of having "no time at all" to much worse periods of reading for several hours a day (to the detriment of the household obviously!). It is almost the dinner hour now; the curfew knells the toll of parting day, the wee small hours draw on apace, and Sam little dreams that an afternoon of Jane Austen is the direct cause of canned tuna for supper…but with a few hardboiled eggs and some curry I'll endeavor to keep him from guessing the real state of the day's events. Ah subterfuge!

Rancho Calera Round-up

The annual Rancho Calera round-up was a much-anticipated event for us children. Each Mother's Day, Jo Chapman invited coast residents to the annual calf-branding and barbeque, giving coast mothers an excuse to gather outdoors in the coast's riotous spring. With our parents busy catching up on others' news or setting up the scattered picnic tables with great bowls of potato salad and cakes, we children were left on our own to thrill to the dust and shouts and lassos, the lowing cows, the flung saliva, the bawling calves laid down wild-eyed and black-tongued in the dust by the quick-working cowboys on horseback. We'd stare between boards of the wooden fence as the cowboys sank the sizzling brand into the calf's flank and then slit the scrotum to remove the white "mountain oysters," tossing these into a bucket to barbeque later. Our noses crinkled with the acrid smell of burned hair and flesh. It was wild and wonderful, guaranteed to keep the attention of the kids.

The teenagers found their own amusements. They'd wander off by themselves in clusters under the scattered oaks or play baseball, using cowpies as bases. The boys blew off excess steam in the hot afternoon by seizing one of the teenage girls and dunking her in the cow trough, a rude sort of honor.

Last weekend we went to the roundup and branding at the Chapman's Rancho Calera, where Frank Trotter is the foreman. The children had the most glorious time watching the cowboys at work, separating the calves from the mothers, branding and castrating the calves…the cowponies are really marvelous to watch in action. There was a fabulous barbecue after the branding; chicken was cooked over a pit of coals, and all the women had brought salads and pots of beans and the cakes that coast women are famous for…the most fantastic creations imaginable. There were kegs of draft beer, too; a memorable occasion.

July 1957

We are having a lovely summer…it is a cool one by our standards (or else we are just getting used to the heat). Sam is still working sporadically on the new addition, and hence everything is in the sort of mess that makes housekeeping quite futile…piles of cement around, tar dripping from the roof on hot days to make a sticky mess on bare feet, small gravel gritty underfoot, sand *everywhere* in the house, sawdust and wood shavings in neat little piles to be waded through as the children come in at meals, lime a delightful play medium for an eager little boy who cannot yet understand its dangers. *Et* cetera. Wheee!

Both the older girls are such swimmers now…Darien is learning to "belly flop" and Jory's dives are beautiful to behold.

[Note: The construction Nan mentions consisted of connecting the main house to the small "guest cabin." When completed, my parents finally moved their bed from the living room corner to a real bedroom.]

August 1957

It seems sad that the summer is over…Jory starts back to school on Tuesday. Once again we must rise at 6:30 and I must wind up my affairs by 3:30 in the afternoon…a very hard thing to manage…but by 4:20 or so when I return from picking her up at the bus it is too late to start any project but dinner. Then too the evenings already seem shorter, and it is darker when we get up in the morning. We have been rising at 7:15 all summer, but it somehow seems much later and more leisurely than 6:30.

[Sam's rainfall record]

Sept. 27	.60"	*Just got back from hunting at Red Mt. Basin. Total: 7. Cool weather.*
Oct. 10	2.00"	*Good soaking rain.*
Oct. 11	.60"	*A wintry October. Sputnik. Stocks decline. On our way to "Rosenkavalier" in rain.*

Heidi reading with Chris and friend Kate

October 1957

Heidi is alarming. She used to be our quiet child, that we viewed with such complacence…it was so pleasant to have a quiet daughter. But no more. Now everything is shrieked at the top of her lungs…she is boisterous, rude, noisy, etc. But at the bottom of it all she is still our Brown Heidi and we are just holding our breaths and treading water and trusting that all will come out all right. She knows more poetry than any child her age I've ever seen, and she spouts it all to Chris as she turns the pages of his books.

* * *

We are grateful for the approach of autumn here, too; there are wonderful cloud formations in the sky and pigeons fluttering out of the madrone trees and a crispness in the air. The highway is deserted, and the coast residents have inherited their earth. Now come the wonderful beach days, with no wind and low tides and the waning year. We shall go clamming soon; I love to think of getting all soaked and cold and gritty with sand and triumphant with a sack of clams.

Tonight we are having pigeon pot pie for dinner and tomorrow we are trying our first roast of wild boar. If it is a success, we are going to save the biggest and most succulent hunk for Christmas dinner.

December 1957

Boys are different from girls. It is something that is hard to describe…it is as though Chris had a wound-up spring inside him all the time which is propelling him into action. He comes out of his room in the morning quite like a ball out of a cannon…jumping stiffly about and shouting just to make noise and because he is so glad to be alive and a man. His two-year-old body is hard and full of constant energy…exactly like a wound-up spring.

January 1958

We have been bursting with New Year's resolutions, but I'm afraid that letter-writing is not to be among them this year. That and fiddle-playing and reading are to suffer, for they are all activities that cannot be indulged in while still keeping the children under reasonable supervision. This year it is to be Long Walks Daily, for the younger children are suddenly at a very mobile age and I am able to get out in the hills with them. We want the children to hike over rugged terrain as automatically as other children might curl up by the TV set or trudge to the kiddy's matinee on Saturday afternoon.

Sam and I are constantly coming up against the matter of "just what kind of children do we want to have" these days; and it is so true that you have to mould them (within their own individual potential, of course) to that goal. And we have decided that we want them to be healthy, active, lovers of the out-of-doors, interested in the arts, widely read, rational, informed, open-minded, polite, poised, sociable, willing to accept responsibility. So here I am marching my small army up hill and down dale each afternoon, and of course they love it; mushrooms are rampant now, and the children are quite familiar with the different varieties; and soon the wildflowers will be springing up…already the woods are dotted with footsteps-of-spring.

It is a good thing not to be housebound, as I have been more or less. But of course Ye Old Earth Mother Nancy also misses having a baby in the cradle; I had always hoped for about six children, but it must be that Nature thinks I have enough.

⁕　⁕　⁕

Everything these days with the little three is "let's pretend." Chris is always the fox or the wolf or the ogre (he calls it "logre"). Heidi also calls him "a noxious"…which is a wonderful noun for him. She has heard me say to him, "don't be obnoxious" when he is swatting his sisters one with a shovel. So now when he attacks her she roars at him, "don't be a noxious, Chris."

February 1958

We have been having almost two weeks of continuous storm conditions. The road is a shambles and there are leaks in our new screen porch, but no leaks elsewhere, thank goodness. It has taken us years to get all the leaks in the room fixed, but at last we seem to be watertight.

This must cease, for I have a mountain of mending to attack…oh dear. I postpone the evil day as long as possible, but it finally catches up with me. *This* is what I hadn't foreseen when I launched into child-raising…I had anticipated the nosebleeds and dentist bills and new shoes

The slide north of Partington

every four months, but I hadn't really faced the matter of who would sew on the buttons and patch the knees and let down the hems. Now Nancy Faces Life. Onward and upward.

*　*　*

Telephones have come down the coast, and we shall probably have one by this summer unless present plans of the telephone company go astray.

March 1958

I and the children went to town on Monday and encountered two bad slides along the highway. We witnessed the first as we were descending the hill north of Post's; it just happened that the highway crew foreman was driving ahead of me down the highway, and I noticed he was craning his neck upward at a steep bank and then hastily signaled to me to keep back. So I stopped, and down between his car and mine roared a big slide, mostly red dirt but some big boulders the diameter of an auto tire. It was quite exciting to see it spill down, and of course it kept coming for ten minutes or so as the rocks above settled themselves in their new locations. And it was lucky that the foreman was there for he was able to clear a narrow passage on one side so I could get by and on into town. And then returning home in the afternoon I found that just half an hour before I arrived a huge slide had poured down just north of the Partington mailboxes and completely blocked the road. A number of cars had collected and the crew with its heavy equipment was trying to make it passable. The children loved watching the big steamshovel trying to grapple with boulders that were the size of a sofa. They had a one-way passage cleared after we had waited three-quarters of an hour or so, and finished clearing it out the next day. Whee! A real coast winter.

* * *

The huge slide just north of the Partington mailboxes closed the highway for a week, Jory stayed with friends so she would not miss school, and we all hiked down Torre Canyon to get our mail. This afternoon we shall go to pick up Jory and bring her home...we have seemed like a very small family with just the younger three children at home, but I am glad that she didn't miss the week of school.

April 1958

[Sam's rainfall record]

April 1	3.20"	
April 2	2.30"	
April 3	1.25"	*Culvert by dam overflows for first time. Carmel River floods.*
April 4	.80"	
April 5	.20"	
April 6	.90"	*Marooned. 59.30 inches so far this year.*
April 7	1.00"	
April 16		*Now we have a hot spell. Swimming.*

Spring is here with a vengeance...we are all trotting around in shorts and sweltering. All this, of course, after the wettest March and early April in history. We have had, I think, 61 inches of rain, which is our record for the years that we have been here...and of course April and May showers could bring it up an inch or two more. The ridge road is rutted beyond belief.

Now I am bursting with spring fever, which has taken the form of vast plans to renovate the house...I am painting and scouring and making curtains and everything looks so much cleaner and newer. In the garden, I am relentlessly peeling things back to a bare minimum. No flowers, and more grass and berry vines. When people ask me why I don't beautify the place with beds of iris and hanging baskets of begonias I shall point at my children frolicking on the lawn and say, "There are my flowers."

Easter table

* * *

We had a very gala Easter, which is a day that we make a great deal of. We had everything decorated to the hilt for Sunday morning…tiny chicken pies for breakfast and "mock champagne" (pineapple juice and ginger ale in champagne glasses) which the children loved. We also had an egg tree…we hung a manzanita branch with decorated empty egg shells (we had blown out the contents) and it was amazingly beautiful and a great success. We'll add to it every year. The table was a bright mass of bunnies and chickens and decorated place mats (which Jory made last year)…it looked like a spring Christmas.

* * *

Big Sur is beginning to get rather respectable, for as it has gotten more "chic" the prices have risen accordingly and fewer and fewer of the Bohemian element can afford to buy or rent homes here…so the beards and sandals (complete with dirty feet) have moved south to Gorda where a new colony flourishes. And Henry Miller has two cars (one a Cadillac) and plays ping-pong and has become positively bourgeois…his son reads nothing but comic books and his daughter pin-curls her hair at a pink-satin-and-tulle vanity table. Quel malheur! Whither the Left Bank?

* * *

Your letter exhausted me. Don't you people ever just enjoy life?! I (even on school days) read for at least a half hour after the others have left the breakfast table, sipping coffee and enjoying life. And then after lunch we all have another quiet time, each one curling up with his own book, while the younger two children nap. The children become accustomed to these periods of privacy and tranquility and they show remarkable consideration in adjusting to them. After all, there is no reason why life must be lived at a furious pace.

July 1958

I haven't written a letter in months to anybody! I keep making plans to organize my life intelligently and somehow this dream never comes about…things slide from bad to worse. I had thought that as the children grew older it would become easier to organize things, but I find just the opposite to be true. "Cope" is a word that I often mull over with amusement these days; I used to "do" things…now all of a sudden I find myself being satisfied if I can just "cope with" things; and after all there is such a world of difference between "doing" and "coping" that I feel I am not really emerging triumphant. But all mothers must go through these inefficient phases…I am sure that I am not shamefully alone in my household muddle.

By the way, we have a phone now—2664.

August 1958

After tucking the children into bed last night, I went for a twilight stroll out into Torre Canyon to enjoy the last light in the western sky and on my sauntering way home I was buzzed by this rattler just before I got to the parking area…I could hardly make him out in the fading light, but he was black and coiled and sounded as loud as a telephone. I rushed to the house for a flashlight and to the garage for a hoe, but I thrust at him too ineffectually and he slid away into a pile of old tile. So I went to bed, not exactly happy, knowing that in the morning I must once again sally to the fray, as it were. And after breakfast I girded my loins and took hoe in hand, feeling quite like Hector saying farewell to Andromache, and went out to explore the tile…shaking like a leaf by the time I actually started to pry the tiles loose. I didn't hear any buzzing, and it hardly seemed likely that he would have stayed around for all those hours…so I almost decided not to persist, but turned over one last tile and there he was coiled in all his horror. Anyway, he is no more.

* * *

August is *not* our good time of year! Everything piles up, and yet it is too hot even to move…we have been having days in the high eighties, and it is not too much cooler at night.

* * *

Late this afternoon Tirzah Roosevelt invited the girls to tea while the rest of us played music… *there* was an event. The girls were all done up in their finery and Tirzah sailed out to meet them with very proper handshakes when we arrived. The party was a rousing success. All sorts of goodies were served…including hot chocolate with whipped cream and Swiss candies and rare crackers (digestive biscuits and such) and small gifts were presented and opened amid loud shrieks of delight (Tirzah actually presented them with trinkets preserved from her own childhood…a heart locket for Jory, a perfume bottle for Darien, and a tiny purse for Heidi with five pennies in it). Then Tirzah opened her closets and got out all her finery and let the girls dress up in it…filmy peignoirs, velvet dressing-gowns, satin nightgowns…the girls minced and paraded and shrieked and giggled…and I gather that Tirzah enjoyed it more than anyone else. When we were through playing, the four of them emerged, drunk with chocolate and absolutely reeking of Darien's new perfume.

* * *

Sandy's garbage dump caught on fire and great excitement reigned for a while; Sam was away from home…he was hunting up on the ridge with the head forest ranger here. I was the first to spot the fire, aside from Sandy himself who has no phone, so I hastily called in the fire and asked them to rush the fire crew there…they did so and also contacted the forest ranger by radio in his truck and announced that there was a fire at Angulo's…you can imagine how Sam and he raced along the ridge to get here…they came down the fire-break that was bull-dozed this spring down upper Partington arriving at Sandy's five minutes before the pump-truck. They found the fire spreading badly, but the pump crew got it under control.

It proved an excellent fire drill for all of us. A friend was staying with us, and we sat together trying to anchor each other on the rooftree of the house, one of us not being enough to hold the hose, wetting down all the oaks and pines and shouting orders to the children to turn on all the various sprinklers with smoke filling the air and making us all cough and weep (a few of the tears being doubtless because of our own fury at our woman's weakness). What an experience trying to wet down the place and also keep the children calm while the smoke in the air is pumping adrenaline through our systems and trying to do exactly what Sam would wish me to do…so many things to think of at a moment when one is so unequipped to think!

* * *

Then this weekend we had more alarums and excursions. You may have gotten in on that big electrical storm last night, but I am sure you cannot have had the display that we had. It started far out at sea about 8 in the evening, and we all marveled at it and then went to bed…Sam left about 9 p.m. to sleep down at Keith's cabin, for the two of them were going for a 5 a.m. hunt and he didn't want to disturb me early in the morning. But about 2 a.m. the lightning moved in to the coast and it was really something watching it approach from about twenty miles south…I have never *seen* such a line-storm. I sat up on our couch by the window in our bedroom, because it seemed impossible to sleep…when the September hills are so tinder-dry the idea of lightning is anything but cheering. Sam came up the hill about 3 a.m. because it was beginning to rain and he felt worried about being away from home. So we sat together and watched the display, and about five minutes after he arrived we saw a big bolt hit the spur ridge that runs down into the middle fork of Partington and a fire started…it was an astounding thing to see and yet somehow it had been exactly what I had been expecting and waiting up for. We phoned the woman who takes the fire calls all summer, and she sent the pump crew out right away, but from where they drove on top of the high ridge they were unable to see where the fire was burning and were really unable to get to it because of the brush. We saw their searchlights on top of the ridge trying to locate the fire, but by this time the P.G. and E. had failed us and with no electricity they couldn't be reached by radio and get instructions as to exactly where the fire was. But fortunately rain was falling all this time and though it didn't put out the fire it kept it from spreading too much. So Sam climbed up to the spot with some tools as soon as it was light and dug a fire-break all around it. So now we are all in one piece, but I shan't forget *that* storm very soon.

[Sam's rainfall record]

> *Sept. 7*   *.50"*   *Heaviest electrical storm to date. Watch lightning strike tree, start fire across canyon. Rain and S.H. put it out. Hot deer season. Bucks scarce. (2) 10th anniversary. Darien starts school tomorrow. Good Nevada hunt. Warm weather.*

September 1958

At last the great day has arrived…Darien marches off to her first day in school tomorrow, and she is thrilled. Her shoes are polished (not new, alas, but one must draw the line somewhere) and clean socks are laid out and great discussions have been held between the two young ladies of the house as to "what to wear" *and* a new lunch pail stands resplendent and well-filled in the refrigerator.

How do city mothers adjust to having their little ones in nursery school? I find it catastrophic that they must leave home at age six…goodness knows, this house is going to be a tomb with just the two little ones in it during the day.

November 1958

This letter must cease, for it is dinnertime and, among other things, Chris has just spilled a bottle of ink on the rug. Thank goodness we hadn't yet gotten around to getting a new rug! The villain has been plunked into the tub, and his clothes are soaking in the sink, and we are furious with him. Sam is back in the hills, Jory and Darien are "bopping" together to the dance music that is allowed on Saturday evening, and Heidi is stark naked and insists that she is quite warm enough, thank you, though the rest of us are bundled as befits an early November evening. So you can picture this charming little family vignette….

January 1959

School was closed Monday because the electricity was still off from Sunday's storm (I am becoming a fabulous fireplace cook, now that we have electricity, for I am always stoveless as soon as it rains!). There were lots of big branches down on the road, and Big Sur roofs had suffered during the storm. One neighbor had all his tarpaper torn off and consequent terrible damage to his furniture. Our bathroom skylight blew off, flooding the bathroom, and the tarpaper blew off our pool cabana, but otherwise we were all right.

We love winter here. Of all possible seasons it is our favorite. When it rages outside (and it *does* rage) we feel most snug and warm and cozy. It almost seems as though Big Sur tests those who want to live in it by its wild winters; for those who leave almost always leave because of the winters…they become frightened by the quietness of an isolated hearthside and the terrible noise of the wind outside and the trees that fall across the roads and the violent slides that block the highway. If you really love Big Sur you love these things most of all…we feel rocked in a cradle of safety in the midst of the tempests.

* * *

I am doing lots of wonderful reading with the girls; it is an endless pleasure, and it is so rewarding to see their minds and imaginations sprouting in all directions. This business of child-raising is an endless delight; I feel a constant challenge, not to turn them into some specialized thing that I want them to be, but to mould them into constructive human beings who will be a joy to themselves and to those around them; their interests can be their own, but at least we can train their minds and give them healthy bodies and attitudes.

February 1959

Our living room has changed into a setting for *Treasure Island* now…the bed in the corner has been barricaded with pillows to become the stockade; the pouf is the Hispaniola; the stepladder is Spyglass Hill and Jory is standing atop it wielding a long cardboard tube which represents a telescope. Heidi is "wounded" and Darien has bandaged her within an inch of her life in the stockade…Chris also sports several bandages, but is out with his bow and rubber-tipped arrows doing what he calls "shooding nanimals" for food in the stockade. Every book we read seems to offer possibilities for endless games afterward, and Stevenson (finished last week) really rang the bell…we live amid a welter of piratical phrases and songs.

April 1959

Jory and Darien are so eager to grow up…they look forward to lipstick and bras (of all horrors!) and "tight skirts." They feel deprived because they cannot wear skirts below their knees.

Chris and Heidi roam about the fields and woods much more than Jory and Darien ever did at that age. They walk down over the hills to play with our neighbors' little girl (a mile by road, and they usually follow the road) and then they walk back again at lunchtime. And they have favorite spots in the woods where they like to play house…they lug all their dolls and Teddy bears there and Chris also carries his tools so that he can "build a house" for them. I am afraid I am perhaps too unprotective a mother, but I love to see them feeling at home in the wilderness. The only danger is from snakes, and both Heidi and Chris are very cautious about them…I know they would immediately retreat from any they came across.

May 1959

Sam is off on a men's picnic today with Nick, David and Harry Dick…no wives were invited because the main reason for the outing was to get Harry Dick away from his wife-sitting responsibilities…an old friend of his and Shanagolden's is visiting with him right now and she is going to stay home with Shanagolden and let him have a few hours off. So Nick, the redoubtable chef, is providing a sumptuous lunch and many bottles of excellent wine, and the four men are going to "have a ball."

Heidi and Chris playing in the meadows

Pfeiffer School circa 1960

* * *

Spring has been lovely here, though dry. Every morning after Sam and the girls have left to meet the school bus at 7:30 I take my last cup of coffee out on our bedroom deck and sit in the early sunshine purring like a cat and reading *The Brothers Karamazov*. It seems at these moments (and indeed at most moments these days) as though life could hold no greater joy.

June 1959

It has been fearfully hot...the berries are withering on the vine before they really ripen...and none of us seem to have much energy. We are accustomed to hot weather in August and September, but somehow it doesn't seem right to have a sizzling June.

You spoke of getting off the merry-go-round, but it seems to me that the closing of school just put me *on* it. Things have been absolutely chaotic since the middle of June...friends dropping in, gayeties, barbeques, beach excursions, etc. I pant for a few solid hours of reading sans interruptions.

August 1959

Harry Dick was up with us in the Sierra for two weeks during July…he had just put Shanagolden in a rest home…a step he has simply had to face if he is to earn a living for him and her…and of course it was a tremendous emotional crisis for him. We were all glad that he joined us for that period, and it meant a great deal to him. Harry Dick made Chris a beautiful stone tomahawk, and he also made a complete wooden village for the girls (all done just with an axe) and the camp is quite a children's lair.

* * *

I begin now to think with sorrow of the starting of school right after Labor Day…the only bright note is that the tourist traffic on the highway also will stop at that time…there are more people here than ever this year, so that one hates to drive in to town, and I suppose we have *Life* magazine to thank for that. But at least they don't wander up our hilltop (they can't…we have the lower gate locked) and up here at home all seems as quiet as ever. I find I like the human race most when I don't have to see too much of it…an antisocial attitude, I admit, but I imagine that many of the world's great minds might agree with me, so at least I feel myself in rather good company! Fortunately, as should be, the children all love the human race dearly…I think that the desire to escape from it is something that comes upon us with age. It is the natural fruit of contemplation.

[Sam's rainfall record]

Sept. 18 4.10"	*Ah, what a fine entry. Lights out. Writing by flashlight. A real winter storm—and we need it. A very dry season. This will help things out.*
Sept. 19 5.65"	*Absolutely astounding! Tussled with plugged culverts.*
Dec. 22 .40"	*The hottest, driest, longest drought in my memory. All the grass dried that the Sept. storm brought up. Pigeons gone.*

December 1959

The girls' piano lessons progress very well…Darien is doing better than Jory at the moment, but that may not necessarily last. Her insecure early touch has developed into the most delightful of "light" touches…if this continues, she should be a fine Mozart pianist. Darien quite naturally watches the music and lets her hands find their place…*that* is a gift for a beginner.

* * *

I can certainly see how different I have become from the person I was four or five years ago. This raising of children is the best possible discipline for the character, the nerves, and the emotions. Certainly when you think about it discipline is the only thing that will ever create anything of value, and it is very true that children need a great deal of it…not punishment, but guidance to help them to discipline themselves.

January 1960

You can see that this is wintertime. Always Shakespeare in the winter and in the summer, Jane Austen in the fall and George Meredith in the spring. Sam deplores this squirrel-cage aspect of my literary life. Actually, I vary the diet, in spite of what he says. He has just suffered with me through all of the Brontes' works (when every cough, however slight, put me on the rack), and now the poor lamb must endure my epileptic agonies as I plunge into Dostoyevsky's *The Idiot*. Everything is violent now…I rage, pale, whisper with horror, shriek convulsively, pound the table, weep. Any husband in his right mind would be glad…nay, joyful…to get his wife back to an English stroll with Emma and Mr. Knightly around a decorous shrubbery.

June 1960

That Time of year is here again…we swelter in weather that starts the day at 80 degrees but climbs well toward 90 by suppertime; my hair is always in my eyes because I *will* swim without a cap; the girls have an acute shortage of summer dresses, but where will I sandwich in the sewing session?…three pink dresses are under way but bogged down. The children chafe because school continues until the 17th. The last two weeks have been one whirl of activities…the school play-day and graduation, a retirement party for Darien's teacher, picnics of one sort or another. This weekend looms whirlish with a huge picnic and swimming party (at our home) honoring our local mailman, who drives past Partington Ridge every day but has never yet been up it…twenty children, at least twenty adults, ham, potato salad, olives, pickles, numerous bee-stings, and several near-drownings, but everyone having a ball as it were. (You see how familiar I am with these events: I can predict every item of it in advance!)

[Sam's rainfall record]

> After two low rainfall years the springs are lowest ever. My pipeline runs about enough for two sprinklers. The summer weather was pleasant with a lot of high fog for those below. No extreme heat in the fall. Hottest in July (98°). But water is mighty scarce. The South Fork of the Big Sur River was dry above Pick Creek for the first time in my memory.

A high fog

December 1960

Clem and Emile keep pouring salt on my wounds as they junket about the world. In November they sent a gorgeous fat program from the Met in New York with "wish you were here" scribbled on it. Then came postcards and letters from Viareggio, where they have a studio in the Via Puccini. Today a very fat envelope arrived, and I wailed to Sam "I just know it's from the Vienna Staatsoper" and sure enough, it was, with some fiendish scribbling from Emile on the cover of the opera program ("Nancy—stop your washing—put down your sewing—hang up your skillet—leave your husband—send the children off to an orphanage—and come to Wien—it's worth it"). Aren't they beasts? If I ever cross the threshold of the Staatsoper I know I shall die of joy…such a gorgeous old rococo building.

January 1961

I was terribly depressed by the Tolerton's separation…it seemed like the first chink in the ramparts. I wonder what people have in their mind's eye…does some rosier vista stretch ahead? Perhaps I am a coward, but I should shrink inwardly from launching upon the lonelier route. It takes so long to learn to live happily with one person, and then the happiness after all the struggle is so great, that I think it is really easier and richer to grow old together. It is so marvelous to know someone of the opposite sex right down to the very core (and of course one never gets quite to the core).

March 1961

Heidi continues to astound her teacher. Today she marched off to school with a book which she was going to "share" with her class. It is a poetry collection which we gave her for Christmas, and she is going to read aloud out of it Shakespeare's "Full fathom five thy father lies," which she adores. Now that ought to be calculated to send her teacher to bed for a week…first-graders just aren't supposed to do these things! When Heidi gets to the third grade she will probably be "sharing" a treatise on calculus.

* * *

Darien is working hard at her piano study. She really plays very well. We are so fortunate to have Gene to study under. He has the blessed combination of traits which make for the best teaching…his personality is pleasant and kindly so the children all adore him, and yet at the same time his standards are very high and he demands the best in their performance. When it comes to making music, he stands for no nonsense. So Darien loves him dearly, and works like a dog for him. She is quite well aware that he has cast off students who *didn't* work hard (that is, in his private piano teaching) and she is determined that he shall never cast her off. He gives her lots of scales and arpeggios and music theory, and she is really getting a superb musical background.

* * *

I heard from a college classmate that she has become a member of a firm selling insurance and real estate, and I was so happy for her. She is just the sort of woman that all the articles have been written about lately…you know what I mean, the college graduate who wastes her sweetness on the desert air of housewifery and baby-tending and such trivialities. These articles always leave me slightly gasping, for I am the woman (very rare, they tell me) who can find complete fulfillment in home and children…my sights are apparently not as high as they should be.

I think we all have to do what we are cut out to do in this world. For myself, I couldn't possibly envision the selling of real estate as equal to the excitement of raising bright children. And spending time with them. But then my attitude is conditioned by my recognition of my personal limitations as far as energy is concerned…I know that I couldn't do both jobs well, and the one seems more important to me.

* * *

Chris, at five, is turning to the man's world completely, totally absorbed by tools and mechanics and masculine pursuits. I find that my major bête noire in the raising of a son is that dreadful matter of Pockets. Somehow pockets have never become an issue with the girls…they scarcely seem to know they exist. But with Chris pockets are the be-all and end-all of existence. His jeans fall to the floor at night with a resounding clank, and when I pick them up they weigh at least five pounds...it is all the Pockets...they are stuffed to the brim with knives, bullets, pliers, small tractors, nails, marbles...really it would be easier to list what isn't in them. And an issue is made each night when I tell him he must put these jeans in the wash and lay out a clean pair for the morning, for each pocket has to be carefully emptied and the contents stowed in the pockets of tomorrow's jeans. The production exhausts me! And the dirt that boys can accumulate on their clothes! When I feel low in my mind about it I think of all those poor mothers who have three or four of them, and it makes me feel much better.

But he really is a delightful boy. The other day I found him sharpening a tool very industriously, and I said, "You'd better not get that axe too sharp." Chris looked up at me utterly incredulous, as though to say, "How old, how female, and how ignorant!", and said, "This isn't an *axe*. This is a hatchet!" Well, now I know.

* * *

Here it is summery again. Too bad for the water supply, but we try not to think of that and just enjoy it for the moment.

The children are in the throes of fort-building, and they have joined forces with the Bradford children from lower on the ridge and the Morganrath children, who are living at Sandy's now, and have formed two armies. This weekend they built their two forts (which are about a half-mile apart) and made swords and flags and such, and now they are mapping out strategy for wars which are to be held in the future. What with all the running up and down the hills between the two forts, and trotting down to the Healeys and to Sandy's innumerable times they must have covered twenty miles a day easily. Their energy exhausts me. Of course when I try to put that energy to some practical use they always profess to be much too exhausted to dry a dish. The way with children since the world began.

* * *

Yes, that was Sam that Henry was writing about. But Henry's judgment of the human race is so poor in general that one can derive no sweetness from his praise. He is just as apt to praise Mary Baker Eddy and Aimee Semple McPherson and Al Capone. Henry has always been a great admirer of Sam, but I am sure that I, being a member of the lesser sex, do not stand so high in his estimation. Henry doesn't like women, in spite of the fact that he has made abundant use of them all his life. He doesn't think they are people. He likes them to function as squaws, slaves, ornaments and concubines, but they just aren't people and he doesn't like them to get any such erroneous, uppity notions. Even his daughter, adored as the most enchanting of little doll-playthings during her childhood, was promptly set aside as of no value once she turned into (ugh) a Woman. Oh well. Henry may get his own back some day. Right now he is in Europe,

Miller's Description of Sam

The following passage is from Miller's *Big Sur and the Oranges of Hieronymus Bosch*, which is an entertaining and rambling discourse on Miller's experience in Big Sur.

There is one young man in this community who seems to have espoused the kind of wisdom I refer to. He is a man with an independent income, a man of keen intelligence, well educated, sensitive, of excellent character, and capable not only with his hands but with brain and heart. In making a life for himself he has apparently chosen to do nothing more than raise a family, provide its members with what he can, and enjoy the life of day to day. He does everything single-handed, from erecting buildings to raising crops, making wines, and so on. At intervals he hunts or fishes, or just takes off into the wilderness to commune with nature. To the average man he would appear to be just another good citizen, except that he is of better physique than most, enjoys better health, has no vices and no trace of the usual neuroses. His library is an excellent one, and he is at home in it; he enjoys good music and listens to it frequently. He can hold his own at any sport or game, can vie with the toughest when it comes to hard work, and in general is what might be called "a good fellow," that is, a man who knows how to mix with others, how to get along with the world. But what he also knows and does, and what the average citizen can not or will not do, is to enjoy solitude, to live simply, to crave nothing, and to share what he has when called upon. I refrain from mentioning his name for fear of doing him a disservice. Let us leave him where he is, Mr. X, a master of the anonymous life and a wonderful example to his fellow-man.

enjoying himself and basking in the attentions of a very young lady (his letters to ridge friends suggest that she is so young that anywhere except in France she would be considered San Quentin quail). So perhaps Henry is right, and women are really fools. They must be. How else can one explain all these sweet young things who move in with Picassos and Millers and even (God help us) T.S. Eliots? Leave us hope that the young Hopkins ladies will be a bit more shrewd!

Farewell for now. Our neighbor's son, who walked up the hill today to work on the fort with the girls, is going to carry this letter to the mail for me.

April 1961

We are sweltering here in summer heat, and I imagine it is the same in Berkeley. We breakfasted at 7 this morning, with all the doors wide open and the thermometer standing at 72 degrees in the shade. Of course in summer this would seem unseasonably cool to us, and we'd probably be pulling on sweaters, for we get so acclimated to our temperatures in the high eighties, but at the beginning of April this first warm weather leaves us all limp and panting.

May 1961

So what do we think of life halfway through it? We'd probably say that we are grateful for blessings that are beyond our own control: we have enough financial security to live simply without much effort, and we have the temperament to be satisfied with simple things and not yearn to compete in the treadmill. We find our greatest joys are comparatively easy for us to come by…fresh air, a warm fire on the hearth, a landscape unobliterated by concrete and human effluvia, a glass of wine, mushrooms from our woods, a good book to read aloud. The children, of course, will grow to other tastes and other desires, and we shall bend every effort to help them fulfill their own natures. We have, as all parents, brought them into the world in a great burst of selfishness and egotism, and our responsibility is to them and not theirs to us.

Seven

"Big Sur is a wonderful education in how to
be tolerant of other ways of life."

The year 1961 marked a major shift in the family. Nan was 35, Sam 46. The oldest child was 11, inching toward teenagerhood. A new six-year-old, Craig, joined our ranks through adoption. These changes in the family were reflected in Nan's correspondence, which became more sporadic, less detailed and generally more rushed. Nan's weekly trios at Nick's became a thing of the past as Nan focused on her growing children.

The world beyond Big Sur was out of joint, fueled by Cold War hostilities. Even in quiet, out-of-the-way Big Sur, the uneasy pressures of the world at large were creeping in. As with schoolchildren all over America, we kids were taught to duck beneath our desks with our hands protecting our heads during periodic emergency "air-raid" drills. For our parents, restless under the strain of constant parenting and saddened by world tensions, it was natural to begin thinking of other more peaceful horizons.

For me, however, this was one of the happiest times of my life. I was finally old enough to be out on my own, and I spent innumerable hours rambling (often barefoot) through the half-mile of woods and grassy fields that separated our house from that of my neighboring friend, Kate. There being nothing to fear, I was free to stay out after dark. I knew every root and rut of the road as well as I knew my own breath and after an evening spent with my friend I could trot back up the road by nothing more than starlight.

May 1961

Exciting news this week…we are adopting a six-year-old lad. We mentioned to you last fall that we were thinking of this, but it was only two weeks ago that an opportunity was offered to us. The upshot of it was that we met and liked Craig, and we brought him home with us and here he has been for seven days now, and we are as thrilled as if we had hatched him ourselves.

You know I have always wanted more children, but Sam feels very sincerely that the population explosion is appalling and we shouldn't do any more to explode it…this way we are not bringing a child into the world but providing a home for a child who is already here and needs care.

* * *

One thing which has cut into my time was the sorrowful sudden death of Tirzah Roosevelt…she had a stroke last Tuesday at the age of 53 and died early Wednesday morning. It was a real and terrible grief for all of us on the ridge, and of course it has been terrible for

Costumes and Our Imaginative Games

Our costumes! How many hours of exuberant play sprang from the dresses and hats and scarves, the harem pants, the clown suits, the swords, the stick horses that filled the heavy old costume trunk. Nan added new costumes each year at Halloween, spending innumerable evening hours at the dining table bent over her fine little Singer sewing machine. We children, mixing bedtime stories and movies in our imaginations, used the costumes to create our own versions of age-old children's games…Darien and Jory's very private and seductive "Princess-Boyfriend" and "Gretchen and Eve" (named after two of Big Sur's beauties); Heidi and Chris's special version of "House" called "John and Susan"; "Animals," in which Craig shone as the leopard who chased the rest of us into trees. Joined by neighbors' children, we starved in rags as wartime "Orphans" and labored hard in our long blue pioneer skirts and bonnets in "Little House on the Prairie." Evenings, we filled the cricket-pulsing sky with whoops and gunshots in "Cowboys and Indians," and our yells of "ollie-ollie-oxen-free" echoed across the canyon when the game of "Hide and Seek" was done.

The most gripping game, played in the dark during summer nights when the hot night wind rattled and banged on the house, was the ever-terrifying "Witch." Darien cloaked herself in black and tiptoed through the dark rooms mumbling and chuckling (a chilling "heh-heh-heh"), pausing to great effect near the favorite hiding spots. I believed so fervently in the game that it was hard to contain my panic and I burst out in screams at her mere approach to the closet in which I crouched.

Craig (left) with Darien and Chris

Nick. The Roosevelts of course had friends all over the world, and the letters have poured in by the hundreds. Oh, it is so sad…Nick plans to stay on here in Big Sur…he feels his life here has deep roots now, but they were such a devoted couple that it will be a very lonely readjustment.

July 1961

Craig is doing beautifully…such a dear child. He and Chris have such a wonderful time together. And he adores the girls, too, and can hardly wait for them to come home from school. All five of them play "house" together…the boys go out hunting to feed the family, and they go to the "office," and the girls tend the children at home and cook and tidy up the house. Jory is moving out of these games, of course…she would rather read now and practice her ballet and such…but Darien still adores playing "house."

Jory is teaching Chris to read, and he is doing very well…he is very proud of his accomplishment.

* * *

Our costume box has swelled to quite exciting proportions over the years. We can delve into it quite confident that we can come up with something for almost any occasion and almost any size.

Water Pipeline

There is no municipal water system in Big Sur. Homes and businesses derive their water from a variety of sources, usually from a spring or a well. There are a number of "mutual water companies," but they are small and their systems not much more than a well, a pump and a tank.

When my father first bought his property, he gained permission to tap into the pipeline that ran across the property on its way down to Jaime de Angulo's ranch. Sam gave Jaime permission to swim in the pool in return for the favor of sharing the water. But when Jaime took liberties with this arrangement—bringing up friends and partying wildly at the pool—Sam sought an independent source of water. He scouted the upper reaches of steep Partington Canyon until he found a spring on the north fork of Partington Creek that was higher in elevation than the property and that had flowing water even in late summer. He applied for the water right and hired the Trotter boys to build a catchment dam and pipeline.

The Trotter-built dam and pipeline still function today. In the photo, modern-day locals Josh Vieregge (left) and Forrest Millington are cleaning silt out of the 60-year-old dam, an every-few-years task. Forrest is a descendant of the original Partington family that homesteaded Partington Ridge.

As for the water, the flow fluctuates during the wet and dry seasons—and during droughts the water flow has been excruciatingly low ("as small as my little finger," my father said)—but to date the spring has withstood every drought since the late 1940s.

August 1961

Deer season starts tomorrow morning and I anticipate six weeks of men-in-my-life. August and September have a flavor all their own here on the coast, when our home is filled to overflowing with men, guns, loading tools, maps, and a general fever of excitement. I have come to enjoy this time of year…it lends a special flavor to the fall…the telephone rings incessantly and it is Kenny or Bob or Keith or Butch or Doug, and there is endless conversation about creeks and draws and knolls and who shot what where. The children adore deer season; they love to help with the butchering and skinning. But with our freezer still holding lots of meat I have given Sam orders to give his first deer away to someone else.

＊　＊　＊

You have probably been thinking that I am no longer among the living, but it is only Summer with a vengeance. A whirl, to say the least…children all about and meals and policing them and hunters in and out. And watering (at this point I couldn't care less if the lawn turns brown).

Jory loved her ballet time in town…they put on a program last night, which went off very well, and Jory did herself proud. She is in a Louisa May Alcott stage, and she wants to shorten her name to Jo. I have always liked that particular name (as who doesn't who has ever loved *Little Women*?) and Jory does seem like a Jo…rather long and coltlike.

October 1961

Our water gets lower and lower. Now if I have two sprinklers going I can't flush toilets too efficiently. Whatever will become of us? Mother says complacently that we can move to town. She doesn't yet realize that *she* isn't going to have any water either. Santa Cruz is already being rationed, and I'm sure Carmel will be next. California is doomed. Sam spent last week building a tractor road for Clem and Emile so that they can put a well 700 feet below their home, alongside the Big Sur River. They have been completely out of water for weeks…carrying it in barrels from down in the Big Sur Valley.

＊　＊　＊

[Sam's rainfall record]

> Oct. 15　*This can't go on much longer or we will have to move out. Temp 90 today. All Central and Southern California in 3rd year of drought. Put in plastic line to help water situation. 2 bucks locally. Nice one near Bridgeport. Craig arrived.*

Jo and Darien each had a friend to spend the weekend. I enjoyed the girls, mad as it was. Girls have such a way of thoroughly enjoying themselves…perhaps they are the "lesser sex" but I must say that they have a ball in their own way. A group of giggling girls has almost more fun than anyone else. They put on a dance program for me, which was notable for the scantiness of the garments worn, and I am afraid that we laughed ourselves into hysterics.

* * *

Having Craig around makes me realize how a country life eliminates fears that are found in city children. He still retains fears which must go far back in his early childhood. It will be interesting to see how long it will be before they are eliminated. The others love to play in the dark, particularly out of doors at night, but Craig is afraid to…he wants the porch light on when he is out at night. And he is timid about tree-climbing, whereas the others will scamper up the trees like monkeys. I'll admit that I have to turn away sometimes when I see Chris shinnying up a long sleek branch of the madrone and getting onto the roof that way; I don't want to instill any fears in him, and yet I myself am afraid to look.

* * *

We have had a veritable blood-bath in our chicken house for several nights…it took us two days to find the hole the coon was getting in. We set a trap last night and caught the villain, and tonight I am going to try coon stew with dumplings for the first time. The old-timers here on the coast always relished coon, so nobody can accuse me of not being adventurous in a culinary way. He was the fattest, healthiest coon we had ever seen (why wouldn't he be after those four chickens?), and we salted and stretched the hide so that the boys can hang it up on their walls.

* * *

We are having gorgeous weather here…clear and sunny but cool, with a viciously white-capped ocean spread out below. *Not* beach weather.

* * *

The Morgenraths have moved away (they had been staying at the Angulo Ranch for over a year now) so the upper ridge seems quiet indeed. Sandy remains, but he is in one of his inebriated periods and always stays home when he is drinking, so no one sees him. Ah, such characters as we have here! Big Sur is a wonderful education in how to be tolerant of other ways of life. Nothing should ever surprise our children in the years to come; I'm afraid they will have seen it all…the good as well as the bad. Actually I think it ought to be advantageous for them to enter college with a broad view of life.

Jo, the dancer

November 1961

Jo and Darien are thriving in their ballet class. They had a ballet test last Monday, and Jo walked off with five stars (out of five possible). Their teacher told her that she "is beginning to look like a dancer," which coming from a teacher not lavish with praise was a great thing indeed.

Jo is taking a serious interest in her schoolwork this year, studying Latin America and finding it stimulating.

January 1962

We went to court for Craig's final adoption procedure, and it was a wonderful experience. We took all the children with us, and the judge was so delightful; I am sure they enjoy adoption cases, for most of their days are spent hearing such sordidnesses. Anyway, he was most inspiring, and the children loved it all. Craig has fitted into the family beautifully; his attitudes have adjusted to ours, and he and Chris have such good times. There is much "silliness" when two boys get together, but then they have to learn to grow up into men. I try to curb them in the major things and let them have their fun in the minor things.

* * *

I am paring our household belongings down drastically, for it is too easy with seven people to get a house like a pack rat's nest. If we haven't used it in the last year, out it goes. We are getting into a wanderlust mood, and I want to be ready to zoom off when the moment is ripe, with as few encumbrances as possible. It's not that we don't like California, but there are times when it seems as though one has been in one place too long.

* * *

Wasn't John Glenn's flight around the earth exciting? Did you listen to the radio broadcast? Sam and I tuned in our radio to listen to the countdown at Cape Canaveral. We intended to turn off the radio once we knew he was in orbit, and then tune in again for the re-entry. But we were absolutely mesmerized and followed him every step of the way, unable to turn our minds to anything else that day. I think it was one of the most emotionally exhilarating events of my lifetime…at those moments you realize what man can do, and it restores one's hopes for the future. I think this is a glorious time in which to live, in spite of all the horrors.

February 1962

Things are already dry here in early February, and our garden is certainly going to be kaput. But it would be insane to try to save it now, only to have it die this summer. We have never had so little water as right now, and of course two months from now there will be that much less.

March 1962

We are having a fierce southern blow today, with intermittent rain. And the worst will probably come tonight…we usually have wind for a day before the rain really starts. But hurray for wet-ness…I cannot get enough of it.

* * *

Today is a bitterly cold March-windy day, following last night's rains…it always seems to me that March is a nice month to stay indoors and look at the world through glass…but things are green and fresh and our daffodils are "taking the winds of March with beauty" …and certainly they have "come before the swallow dares." Isn't Shakespeare really delicious?

May 1962

Jory marched off last night to her first baby-sitting job…down at our neighbors' home. She rode her bicycle down the hill, with her sleeping bag swinging from the handlebars. She gave supper to the three little girls and got them into bed, and then slept there herself. It gave me quite a pang to watch my grown-up daughter sailing off blithely on her bicycle…the end of one era and the beginning of a new one.

* * *

I picked up a cold, and yesterday I wanted to die but managed to survive. I think the reason I have had so many colds this year is my lack of sleep…I try to get to bed early, but then I can't resist reading later than I should, and Darien gets me up at dawn to sit down with her at the piano. She at any rate makes fine progress, though her old mother is a Rambling Wreck. Gene has just started her on Bach…the long-awaited moment. He gave her a prelude this week, and asked me to buy the Two-Part Inventions, so she will be plunging in seriously. She really does remarkably. You would be astounded, considering how frivolous she appears to the outward eye. She is advanced enough now so that she has put "pretty pieces" behind her completely and now has nothing but the real thing…Chopin preludes and Schumann's "Kinderscenen" and some charming early-Spanish sonatinas and now the Inventions. Fun!

June 1962

The children are winding up the school year this week in high spirits and with all sorts of social activities planned…Big Sur has a community picnic at the State Park on the last day of our local school this Friday, with swimming and baseball and a potluck supper out of doors…one of the highlights of the year here in Big Sur. Our children are really fortunate to have spent their early childhood in this kind of small community where everybody knows everybody else…they expect everyone to be friendly, and this is the best attitude toward life, for it usually turns out that people are.

* * *

Auntie Mary made great efforts during this last week to have me meet her religious friend, Ann Ree, and I made just as great (and more successful, it turned out) efforts to avoid any such introduction. She claims that Ann Ree is dying to meet me, and ye olde cynic Nancy knows why: I live in Big Sur, and all the nuts in creation want entrée here. They want to establish a foothold which can lead to information on houses to rent, houses for sale, land possibilities, etc. If you're a friend of someone in Big Sur, it is easier to get "in." I'm getting too old to have to bother about being nice to anyone anymore. The last thing we need on Partington Ridge is Ann Ree and her Recording Angels of the Limmurian Period (pre-Atlantis).

We had such an amusing letter just before Sam left for the Sierra. It came from Ontario, Canada, and was from a gentleman calling himself T. Lobsang Rampa, who is a writer and

Clowning by the pool with the neighbor's kids

slight acquaintance of Henry Miller. How he got our name we'll never know. But Henry of course is abroad, and this gentleman was writing to find how he could get a house in Big Sur. He wanted two or three bedrooms, and it must be near or overlooking the sea. The trouble was, he confessed, he didn't have any money. This is typical, and wouldn't be humorous in itself, except that this Dr. T. Lobsang Rampa (whose stationary proclaimed him to be the author of a number of books on Tibet and Lamaism) was thoroughly exposed as a fraud several years ago, when his first book *The Third Eye* was published…he's a Cockney dockworker or something who had never been near Tibet. So when we received this imposing letter from Dr. T. Lobsang Rampa we were really convulsed; I don't know when we have laughed so hard. I wanted dreadfully to be insulting when I wrote to him, but the native hue of resolution was sickled o'er by the pale cast of thought and I ended up being civility itself. I told him that I would pass his request on to our local real estate person, but assured him that prices here were outrageous and he shouldn't get his hopes up. Now that I think it over, I think that perhaps Big Sur *needs* T. Lobsang Rampa; it takes a rather grandiose, almost Renaissance, imagination to be a fraud on such a large and shameless scale, and to persist in the fraud when everyone knows it is a fraud; perhaps the world would be better off if we had more of these splendid figures.

There are sorrows in this world on a colossal scale, but sometimes it seems as though the laughter rings as resoundingly. I think we'll call two of our next kittens Ann Ree and Lobsang Rampa.

August 1962

It almost seems as though no erstwhile Big Sur marriages remain intact…an interesting study, if one were to go about it. Does Big Sur do this to couples? More likely that certain types of people come to Big Sur. However, for the moment, knock on wood, the Hopkins toddle along with a fair share of sunshine, doing their best to limit the small spots of friction to the Oriental principle of Darkness-in-Light. The older I get, the less surprised I am that so many marriages are unhappy. I am only surprised that any at all are happy. It is really interesting to me how the elements in a marriage that make for eventual happiness are the very elements which you cannot detect or predict at the beginning. We all marry for what seem to us to be good reasons, but if we are happy it is for quite other reasons. I tremble for my children! The most important things, I suppose, are goodwill and an ability to Bend With the Storm…but then there are so many other little factors.

September 1962

School has opened and Jory has changed overnight…a new interest in hairdos has developed, and I, as so many mothers of budding adolescents, am privately appalled by the amount of time that is spent in front of the mirror. She looks hopefully for pimples, viewing them as a badge of grown-up-ness, and this morning she achieved an Italian-style hairdo (by the painful expedient of sleeping all night on rollers) and then was rather alarmed—and a little bit proud—at the result, which was so bushy that I had to spend ten minutes brushing it flat. Oh dear. I see the roller-coaster ride looming ahead, with all sorts of swoops and stomach-sinking drops.

* * *

At last we are planning the trip we have talked about for years, and this November we are heading for New Zealand! This little island has always been our private Hesperides, and we want to go there before the rest of the world discovers it…so far, it is very much off the beaten track. We hope to stay for a year so that the children can have the full year in school.

* * *

Your remark as to the strangeness of doing anything in this "critical time" brought to mind the vast difference between our two generations in this particular respect. Thanks to your first two tranquil decades, you can envision a time which is not critical, but my generation has long

Looking westward

been unable to picture such a thing. We have never been aware of anything but crisis. First it was the Depression, then it was World War II, the Korean War, Suez, the Congo, Berlin, Cuba, the Cold War, bomb testing, etc. If you refer to the stock market as suggesting crisis, we view that as a very minor manifestation. Since life is simply one crisis after another, the idea of abandoning any cherished hopes or plans because of this exterior situation seems absurd. There is no indication that the world one year from now, or ten, or twenty, will be any less critical. So whatever one wants to do one had jolly well do right now.

We are not going to New Zealand as "tourists," believe me. We are simply going to live somewhere else for a year. We want to view the United States from afar, and it will be pleasant to view it from a country that has no international axes to grind and has caused pain to so few people. New Zealand is a tranquil land; life will seem less crucial there, and we may survey our native land's activities with a little less of the moral pressure generated by immediacy. It is impossible to live in the United States and not feel partially responsible for its activities and shortcomings. It will be pleasant to live for a year where people talk about apples and sheep, and where billions are not being spent upon missiles and defense.

* * *

Your wonder at our trip is a curious thing, when this world is so interesting. We really picked this year because it seemed better to go abroad before Jory launches into her high school years and adolescence. We thought this a good year to expose her to another land and another view. They become such rabid conformists during those high school years; this way she will always have stored away in the back of her mind the seed of the idea that there is more than one way to do things and more than one point of view. I agree with Mrs. Kennedy Sr. who once made the comment that her family policy was to put the major effort in on the older children, and that the younger children would follow along. After all, we mothers have only so much strength; but if you get the firstborn children treading the proper paths, their influence will help bring up the younger ones. Certainly, in our family—and in most, I think—the oldest child is a god to the younger ones. Jory is the favorite of each of the younger four...I know because they have all told me that; and consequently her influence on them is tremendous.

To know another people is invariably to sympathize with them; it will not hurt this world at all to have populations moving about getting acquainted with other lands.

Epilogue

O ur family sailed to New Zealand in November 1962. When we returned, in the fall of 1963, the local school system had changed. A new school had been built in Big Sur, with all the modern amenities. Unfortunately, it accommodated only the first six grades; seventh grade and beyond were taught in Carmel. With the bus ride nearly an hour each way to the Carmel schools, my parents tried one year boarding the older two girls in town with a family while the younger three remained in Big Sur (while Darien, a sixth grader, could have remained in Big Sur, she was sent to school in Carmel so that Jory would not board alone). The girls returned each weekend to Partington. But this arrangement proved unsatisfactory, and in the fall of 1964 the entire family moved to Carmel. We returned to Partington for weekends, holidays and long blissful summers.

And so the family moved on. With fewer of the demands and immediacies of small children, Nan began leading weekend high school backpack trips for the Sierra Club and helped edit the first *Ventana Wilderness Guide*. She later served as a founding board member of the Big Sur Land Trust. Sam took up cycling, a passion that he pursued the rest of his life by riding hard, following the racing scene with great interest and seeking out ever lighter cycling equipment. Once we children were out of the house, my parents built a small, gracious home in the Carmel Valley.

Craig returned to Big Sur after high school, and put his adult roots down there. In recent years, he purchased a home in Bradley, inland from the coast. Chris, inspired by weekly Sufi drumming sessions in the 1970s at the neighboring Angulo ranch, took up conga and timbale drumming with his typical, single-minded zeal and later developed a carpentry career. Today, he lives in Carmel Valley and brings his two young daughters down to Partington, where they splash and shriek in the pool as much as we did when young. I graduated from U.C. Berkeley in astronomy, raced bicycles nationally for several years, and then pursued nonprofit environmental work in a variety of locations, including San Francisco and Mono Lake in the rural Eastern Sierra. At present, recently married, I live with my husband at Partington and struggle with thinning out the second-growth forest that sprang up after my father's intrepid woodcutting. Darien majored in music and studied piano at Stanford. Today she shares her musical talent as a piano accompanist for children (that is, when she is not off rock climbing or skiing in New Mexico's mountains, where she lives). She and her Yorkshire-born husband have a son, who annually convenes a weeklong "twenty-something" gathering at Partington for his wide set of college friends. Jory fulfilled Nan's travel dreams. She moved in her 20s to Brazil, where she continues to live today raising and milking goats on a remote farm in a rural mountain area of interior Brazil. She almost never returns home.

My father's interests changed over time from those that first attracted him to Big Sur. In his later years Sam found the place too buggy or too hot or too cold for anything other than a short visit. My mother on the other hand retained her deep love for her home on Partington Ridge. Throughout her life she returned to her mountaintop, where she battled cobwebs, tackled weeds and most often surrendered for hours on the lawn, warmed by the sun, lulled by the incessant hum of natural life around her and transported by an endless succession of books. She spent her final years at Partington and died peacefully in the redwood-paneled home where she had been a bride.

The home on Partington Ridge has remained a family home—a beloved gathering place where we children meet as a family for holidays, where friends come to visit and where each of us spends time refreshing the spirit.

✳ ✳ ✳

Partington Ridge continues as a community, more populous but in many regards little changed from 50 years ago. Where in the 1950s there were perhaps 10 homes, now there are roughly 50, some little more than caretakers' trailers tucked away along the three miles of narrow, winding road. The road itself is little changed other than being sunk ever deeper and broader into the land. Neighbors still gather for holidays and celebrations, gossip out of car windows as they squeeze by each other on the road, share garden produce and, despite many differences, band together in emergencies. Other generations of children have grown up on the ridge, and the hills resound with their games and dreams and delights.

Mary Lu Torén, a long-time Partington Ridge resident, riding on the ridge; 1989 oil painting by George Choley.

Index of Big Sur Residents